# You Can Grow Up In Christ!

# Contents

# Foreword

Have you ever wondered what it takes to make a healthy church? In Ephesians 4:17–32, Paul says that a healthy church practices truthfulness, generosity, and forgiveness. A thriving church deals with anger correctly and seeks to edify its members. This study will teach you how to become part of a healthy church.

Whether going through this study on your own or with a group, hold on as you take this first step in learning how to grow up in Christ and begin your journey of becoming the healthy Christian God wants you to be.

# Introduction

When I began pastoring in 1989, I was a deeply wounded young man. I grew up with an abusive, alcoholic father and carried those emotional scars into the ministry. Fortunately, God has miraculously worked to heal me from many of those scars. Now, I'm a much healthier husband, father, and pastor.

As a pastor, it has become one of my greatest passions to use the lessons I learned to help other Christians. I desire to see fellow believers become spiritually and emotionally healthy because a spiritually and emotionally healthy person is much more likely to get and stay involved in building God's kingdom. I've filled this book with the tools God used to help me, and I hope He will also use them to help you.

I wrote this book to be both informational and transformational. If you do what it says, the lessons from God's Word can transform your life. You can use this book individually or as a small group study (There is a Leaders Guide in Appendix D). Each chapter contains real stories about people who dealt with these issues in their own lives. The stories are true. However, the names and details are changed to protect people's privacy. There are callout boxes to help you apply the material to your life and exercises, quizzes, and discussion questions for personal reflection and small groups. Please use them.

May God bless you as you seek to grow up in Christ!

# 1

# You Can Grow

## 1. God designed you to grow up in Christ

*"And He Himself gave some to be apostles, some prophets, some evangelists, and some pastors and teachers, for the equipping of the saints for the work of ministry, for the edifying of the body of Christ, till we all come to the unity of the faith and of the knowledge of the Son of God, to a perfect man, to the measure of the stature of the fullness of Christ; that we should no longer be children, tossed to and fro and carried about with every wind of doctrine, by the trickery of men, in the cunning craftiness of deceitful plotting, but, speaking the truth in love, may grow up in all things into Him who is the head—Christ—from whom the whole body, joined and knit together by what every joint supplies, according to the effective working by which every part does its share, causes growth of the body for the edifying of itself in love." (Ephesians 4:11–16)*

I met Mary one Sunday morning while pastoring my first church. She became a Christian two and a half years earlier but had trouble finding a church she felt comfortable attending. Something would always make her feel uncomfortable, and she would leave. On the third week she attended our church, Mary decided to visit the Sunday school class before the morning service.

The class started with a time of sharing and prayer requests and then I began my lesson on Romans 3:23, "All have sinned and fall short of the glory of God." Mary told me earlier how she learned about her sin—the things she'd done that broke God's laws—and how Jesus died to pay for her sins so she could find forgiveness.

I continued with the lesson and said we all sin because of Adam's sin's effect on humanity. I read from Romans 5:12, where it says, "Therefore, just as through one man sin entered the world, and death through sin, and thus death spread to all men, because all sinned . . ." Then I looked around at the group and said, "We were all born with a sin nature."

Mary's head popped up. In our previous conversations, she shared how she grew up in a home celebrating humankind's potential. Her college training reinforced this belief, and she chose her career in social work because she believed in every person's potential for good. She said, "You mean to tell me that you think my six-month-old granddaughter is a sinner?"

I answered, "Yes. According to what Paul says in Romans 5:12, she is a sinner." I went on to say that while I believed Mary's granddaughter was too young at six months to be guilty of breaking God's law, as she grew, her sinful nature would exert itself through things like selfishness and lying. She would take things she shouldn't and then lie about it without anyone teaching her how to lie or steal.

Mary's face turned red as her anger grew. She said, "I can't believe my granddaughter is anything but a pure and innocent child." Mary didn't say another word. She left after the Sunday school class and never came back.

I wish this were an isolated incident, but I've seen the same thing happen many times. People agree with the Bible until something in it disagrees with their beliefs. While this type of person doesn't always leave the church, their beliefs often stay the same. I've spent years as a pastor preaching sermons and teaching Sunday school classes geared toward helping Christians grow in their faith. Unfortunately, I have far too often seen people continue in their pre-Christian beliefs long after coming to Christ.

Then in 2010, as I faced a crisis that caused me to evaluate what I was doing as a pastor, I looked closely at what Paul said in Ephesians 4:11–16 about the church, how it should function, and my role as a pastor. According to Paul, God gave apostles, prophets, evangelists, pastors, and teachers to the church so they could equip Christians to do the work of the ministry. Equipped Christians are no longer "tossed to and fro and carried about with every wind of doctrine, by the trickery of men, in the cunning craftiness of deceitful plotting" (Ephesians 4:14).

Instead, equipped Christians "[speak] the truth in love" so they can "grow up in all things into Him who is the head—Christ" (Ephesians 4:15). When Christians are equipped for ministry, they become healthier both spiritually and emotionally. They're victorious over sin, speak the truth in love, and work together to become a healthy church. Equipped Christians grow together and live for Christ in a way that's impossible for them to do by themselves.

The people I "equipped" could do jobs in the church, like teaching a class or leading a small group. But they were still led astray by the same temptations and false beliefs they struggled with when they were first saved. They weren't getting victory over sin or speaking the truth in love as they should, and they weren't working and growing together as God intended. I realized that their failure to grow up in Christ meant I was failing in my equipping. I needed to dig deeper into what it meant to "equip the saints."

The point: God expects you to grow up in Christ. Jesus gave us apostles, prophets, evangelists, pastors, and teachers to help equip Christians for the ministry. Equipping Christians is more than just teaching them how to do a job.

## 2. To grow, you need a plan
*"This I say, therefore, and testify in the Lord . . ." (Ephesians 4:17a)*

Once I realized I needed to improve my equipping, I started searching for how to equip the saints. I looked at Ephesians 4:11–16 again. Paul gives the command to equip, but I didn't see any specifics on how to do it in the passage. I would typically do a word study to see how other Scripture passages use the word, but "equipping" is only used once, here in Ephesians 4:11.

Then I discovered that several external sources from Paul's day used the word equipping in a way that might help clarify its meaning. In the second century A.D., a pharmacist sent a letter to a friend saying he had "made a potion to heal a sick person" by mixing ingredients.[1] The pharmacist described the result as "ready [equipped] to take."[2] According to the pharmacist, "equipping" meant to make something ready for use.[3] When I applied this meaning to the passage, I discovered that "equipping the saints" means making Christians ready for Christ to use so they can do the work of ministry and help the church grow.

My next hurdle was figuring out how to get the saints ready for Christ to use. I found it hard to believe that Paul would give pastors like me the job of equipping the saints without telling us how. I knew the answer must be in Ephesians. I read Ephesians repeatedly, looking for a clear teaching about how I was supposed to equip people. Then, as I was rereading Ephesians 4:17, I was struck by what Paul said: "This I say, therefore, and testify in the Lord." Writers use the word "therefore" to continue their thoughts from the previous section to say, "Since what I said before is true, this is how it should affect you." I realized Paul was completing his thoughts on equipping in verses 11-16. I could almost hear Paul say, "I told you what role equipping is supposed to play in the church, so now I am going to tell you my plan for how to do it."

Once I understood what Paul meant, I was able to break the rest of Ephesians down into five essential areas of equipping:

1. We need to grow up in Christ - Ephesians 4:17-32
2. We need to walk in love - Ephesians 5:1-2
3. We need to let the light of Christ shine in our hearts by dealing with sin in ourselves and the church - Ephesians 5:3-14
4. We need to understand God's will - Ephesians 5:15-6:9
5. We need to stand against spiritual attack - Ephesians 6:10-18

I believe Paul expects every Christian to know and grow in these five areas to be ready for Christ to use in ministry.

The point: Paul gave us a clear picture of what a healthy church is supposed to look like. He also gave us a clear plan for how to make it happen. Equipping is not just teaching Christians how to do a job; it's preparing them for Christ to use. Any Christian can grow up in Christ and become active in creating a healthy church by using Paul's teachings in the book of Ephesians.

## 3. To grow, you need to understand the need for change

*". . . that you should no longer walk as the rest of the Gentiles walk, in the futility of their mind, having their understanding darkened, being alienated from the life of God, because of the ignorance that is in them, because of the blindness of their heart; who, being past feeling have given themselves over to lewdness, to work all uncleanness with greediness." (Ephesians 4:17b–19)*

When you receive Jesus into your life and believe in His work on the cross to pay for your sins, some things may change immediately. God may deliver you from swearing, drugs, or various other sins. You may develop an overwhelming desire to read the Bible or to tell others about your new faith. However, much of who you were before your salvation is still part of you after. That's why Paul says, "You should no longer walk as the rest of the Gentiles walk" (Ephesians 4:17). You need to start changing from who you were into the person God wants you to be.

Paul explains why when he says that the root of the unsaved person's problem is the futility of their mind. The word futility means worthless and is the same word translated as "vanity" in the Septuagint or Greek version of Ecclesiastes 1:2. The Complete Word Study Dictionary describes futility as the emptiness of living for the present versus the fullness of living for the future.[4] Your mind includes your understanding, will, and conscience. Paul is saying that you need to stop living like the unsaved people around you, like the unsaved person you used to be because the unsaved person's understanding, will, and conscience are caught in the trap of living for the emptiness of the present physical world and ignoring the future of eternity.

The unsaved person's mind is futile because their understanding—their perception of reality—is darkened and deprived of the light of God's truth.[5] This doesn't mean unsaved people are incapable of understanding anything. If that were the case, then unsaved people could never discover anything about the world around them. No. Their darkened understanding makes them draw the wrong conclusion whenever the evidence points to God.

I wanted to be a paleontologist when I was young. Dinosaurs and evolution fascinated me. I wanted to spend my life looking for Darwin's missing links. Even after believing in Jesus, I wanted to study dinosaur bones and learn how evolution worked through millions of years to create life on Earth. I didn't know it, but my darkened understanding from before my salvation influenced my thinking.

Eventually, I learned what the Bible says about life and how it began. I read in Genesis 1 and other places in the Bible that God created all life on earth in 6 days. I had a choice. I could continue believing what I learned before being saved, or I could take God's word and believe the Bible. I chose not to accept what the people who always draw the wrong conclusions about the facts when they point to God said and believed God and His Word instead. Now I read magazines with articles written by reputable scientists that show scientifically that the earth is thousands and not billions of years old.

Since your understanding was darkened before you were saved, you also drew wrong conclusions about God and the world around you. What do you think about the possibility that your understanding of some things may still be wrong?

_____

_____

_____

The unsaved person's mind is also futile because it is "alienated from the life of God" (Ephesians 4:18). When God created Adam and Eve, He created them to live for Him. However, when they sinned, they lost the ability to live in a way that pleased Him. Now their descendants, the unsaved people of the world, can't live the life God intends because their alienation from God drives them to live a life God doesn't want.

Paul explains why the unsaved person's alienation from God drives them to live apart from Him. First, their ignorance, which comes from their lack of understanding about how to live for God and about the punishment living apart from God brings, leads them to commit evil deeds.[6] Second, the "blindness of their heart" keeps them from seeing the goodness of God and trusting in the one person, Jesus, who can take away their ignorance. Paul talks about this blindness of heart in 2 Corinthians 4:3–6:

> But even if our gospel is veiled, it is veiled to those who are perishing, whose minds the god of this age has blinded, who do not believe, lest the light of the gospel of the glory of Christ, who is the image of God, should shine on them. For we do not preach ourselves, but Christ Jesus the Lord, and ourselves your bondservants for Jesus' sake. For it is the God who commanded light to shine out of darkness, who has shone in our hearts to give the light of the knowledge of the glory of God in the face of Jesus Christ.

Where was your life headed when you put your trust in Christ?

_____

_____

_____

Finally, the unsaved person's mind is futile because it is past feeling (Ephesians 4:19). The word for past feeling comes from the words "out of" and "to smart."[7] It's where we get the English word analgesic or painkiller. "Past feeling" means the unsaved person's ability to see the difference between right and wrong is deadened. Their conscience is numb to the sense of honor and shame God put in each of us when He created us as moral beings.[8]

This numbed sense of right and wrong leads them to act out in lewdness (Ephesians 4:19) or a lack of moral restraint.[9] They're driven by a desire for sinful pleasure, which often includes arrogance and insolent words.[10] The unsaved person's numbed conscience also draws them toward both uncleanness—physical and moral filth, and greediness—the longing of people who have forsaken God to fill themselves with the lower objects of nature.[11] You don't need to look far in Hollywood, on TV, or in the news to find lives consumed with lewdness, uncleanness, and greediness.

What acts of lewdness, uncleanness, or greediness did you think were "okay" before you were saved?

_____

_____

_____

Unfortunately, the futile mind you had before you received and believed in Jesus still holds countless ideas and beliefs that contradict the understanding God wants you to have, the life God wants you to live, and the conscience God intended to guide you. You need to change even if you grew up in a Christian home, received and believed in Jesus as a young child, attended church, or a Christian school.

The futility of the darkened understanding, alienated life, and deadened conscience of the unsaved mind have affected all the unsaved people who influenced you before you were saved and still affects the unsaved people who try to influence you now. Even Christians whom the unsaved futile mind has influenced can influence you with thinking tainted by futility.

The point: When you receive Christ and believe in His work on the cross to pay for your sin, God gives you everything you need to grow. However, you won't grow and be ready for Christ to use if you don't understand your need for change. God says you need to change because the futility of the unsaved mind has influenced your understanding, drive in life, and conscience. Whether your futile thinking comes from things you concluded for yourself, were taught by unsaved people, or learned from Christians influenced by unsaved people, there are things you need to change.

## Conclusion

Christ has given you—Christian—the plan and the people (apostles, prophets, evangelists, pastors, and teachers) you need to make you grow and be ready for Him to use. The first step in preparing you for use is helping you understand the need for change. You must change because the world's darkened understanding, alienation from God, and moral deadness have shaped you. The person you were needs to be replaced by the person God wants you to become.

Discussion Questions:

1. Do you have any thoughts or questions about this chapter?

2. What were you like before you were saved?

3. What did you believe about God before you were saved?

4. How did your environment shape your beliefs about God and the world around you before you were saved?


5. What have you read in the Bible that you disagree with?


6. What would you like to gain from this study?

# 2

# It's Time to Change

*"But you have not so learned Christ, if indeed you have heard Him and have been taught by Him, as the truth is in Jesus: that you put off, concerning your former conduct, the old man which grows corrupt according to the deceitful lusts and be renewed in the spirit of your mind, and that you put on the new man which was created according to God, in true righteousness and holiness." (Ephesians 4:20-21*

## 1. Learning Christ starts with the Gospel

*"But you have not so learned Christ, if indeed you have heard Him and have been taught by Him, as the truth is in Jesus" (Ephesians 4:20-21)*

Paul uses a curious phrase in Ephesians 4:20 to explain why we shouldn't live like unsaved people anymore. He says, "But you have not so learned Christ." To understand what the "not so" part means, you must understand what it means to "learn Christ." The best way to explain this is to use my own experience. I "learned Christ" when my family attended a small church in the suburbs of Chicago. I was about five years old, and my only memories of the church are the white siding and dark wooden pews that were hard to sit still in. One early spring morning, my Sunday School teacher took our class over the railroad tracks to a nearby convenience store to buy treats before the morning service.

While all the other children were picking out their favorite candies, I realized I had no money. I asked the teacher if she would buy me something, but she said no. So, I stealthily grabbed an ice cream bar and put it in my coat pocket. When we left the store, I pulled out the ice cream bar and started to eat it.

My teacher came over and asked where I'd gotten the money to buy the ice cream bar. My cheeks started to burn, but I lied and said I'd found money on the floor in the store. By the time we got back to the church, I felt terrible. At the end of the service, as he did every week, the pastor called all the children to the front of the church to sing "Into My Heart" by Henry D. Clarke. I still remember the words:

> Come into my heart, Lord Jesus;
> Come in today, come in to stay,
> Come into my heart, Lord Jesus.[1]

As we sang the song, I knew I was guilty of stealing and lying and deserved God's punishment, but I also understood I could be forgiven if I believed in Jesus and let Him come live in my heart. While singing, I prayed and asked Jesus to forgive me and come into my heart.

When you "learn Christ," your Gentile mind, with its darkened understanding, alienation from God, and moral deadness, is confronted with the person and work of Jesus Christ through the Gospel. Paul explains the Gospel in 1 Corinthians 15:1–5:

> Moreover, brethren, I declare to you the gospel which I preached to you, which also you received and in which you stand, by which also you are saved, if you hold fast that word which I preached to you—unless you believed in vain. For I delivered to you first of all that which I also received: that Christ died for our sins according to the Scriptures, and that He was buried, and that He rose again the third day according to the Scriptures, and that He was seen by Cephas, then by the twelve.

The Gospel literally means "good news" and says that Jesus Christ died for your sins, was buried, and rose again on the third day. The Gospel is important because you were born a sinner (See Chapter 1), and as soon as you were old enough, you started sinning. Sin creates a barrier that keeps you from having a relationship with God and ultimately keeps you from heaven. Two things the Bible calls sin are lying and stealing. The Bible says, "Thieves will not inherit the kingdom of God" (1 Corinthians 6:10), and, "All liars shall have their part in the lake which burns with fire and brimstone" (Revelation 21:8). If you've lied or stolen even once, the punishment of not inheriting "the kingdom of God" and burning "with fire and brimstone" applies to you!

Fortunately, God loves you despite your sin and wants a relationship with you. That's why God sent His Son, Jesus Christ. John 3:16 says, "For God so loved the world that He gave His only begotten Son, that whoever believes in Him should not perish but have everlasting life." Forgiveness through Jesus requires two things from you: 1) that you receive Jesus into your life and become a partaker of His life, 2) that you believe in His name (who He is), that He can save you, and that He is the only way to eternal life and heaven (John 1:12).

Something amazing happens when you "hear" the Gospel and receive and believe in Jesus. You don't just hear the person talking to you or see the words you're reading. You hear the voice of Jesus with the "ear of the mind,"[2] and God gives you the ability to be *"taught"* by Him so you can understand that Jesus is the source of the life God intends for you.[3] God also opens your ears to hear the truth that can only be found in Jesus.

When I was five, God opened the ears of my mind to hear the truth that is in Jesus. As we sang "Come Into My Heart," God helped me understand the truth about what I had done when I stole the ice cream bar and lied to my Sunday school teacher. I knew I was guilty and needed God to forgive me. I understood the truth that

God was offering me forgiveness through Jesus. I asked God to forgive me and for Jesus to "come into my heart," as the song said.

The truth I learned the day I was saved—the truth in Jesus—is based on reality and is pure from all error or falsehood.[4] All of the stories in the Bible about how Jesus lived, died, and rose again have been validated over and again by historical and archeological evidence.[5]

Even secular historians testified to the truth found in Jesus. In his work Jewish Antiquities, the Jewish historian Flavius Josephus, written in about 90 AD, refers to the "brother of Jesus, who was called Christ." Then again, in about 110 AD, The Romans Pliny and Tacitus wrote that Jesus "was executed during the mandate of Emperor Tiberius when Pontius Pilate was governing in Judea."[6]

Beyond the physical and historical truth of Jesus, however, is that Jesus is the source of spiritual truth. When Pilate asked Jesus if He was the king of the Jews, Jesus said,

> You say rightly that I am a king. For this cause I was
> born, and for this cause I have come into the world,
> that I should bear witness to the truth. Everyone who
> is of the truth hears My voice. (John 18:37)

The truth of Jesus is that He is "the Christ, the Son of the living God" (Matthew 16:16). Jesus is "the way, the truth, and the life. No one comes to the Father except through Me" (John 14:6). He was "delivered into the hands of sinful men . . . crucified, and the third day rose again" (Luke 24:7) so He could save sinners (1 Timothy 1:15). Now, everyone who believes in Him "will receive remission of [payment for] sins" (Acts 10:43) and "become children of God" (John 1:12).

If you haven't already received and believed in Jesus Christ for your forgiveness, take time now to pray. You can receive God's forgiveness and be freed from the punishment you deserve by praying a prayer of faith. Here's a sample prayer, "God, I know I've committed sins and need your forgiveness. I believe Jesus died to pay my sin debt and that His payment for my sins is the only way to heaven. I receive Jesus into my life. Amen."

The point: You "learn Christ" when you hear what He's done for you through the Gospel. The Gospel tells you what you need to know to be saved. When you "learn" Jesus, God opens the ears of your mind so you can hear the truth that can only be found in Him.

---

Has there ever been a time when you made a decision to receive and believe in Christ through a prayer of faith? If so, when?

_____

_____

_____

---

## 2. Learning Christ opens the door to change

*"But you have not so learned Christ. . . that you put off, concerning your former conduct, the old man which grows corrupt according to the deceitful lusts . . ." (Ephesians 4:20, 22)*

When you trust Christ for your forgiveness, several miraculous things happen. You are born again (John 3:3) and become a child of God. You are guaranteed to get into heaven (Ephesians 1:13–14). Your spirit, which was dead because of the effects of sin, is made alive by the Spirit of God. The Spirit of God makes His home within you, and He makes you a part of the church, which is the body of Christ on Earth. The Spirit of God helps you understand the Bible and gives you the ability to obey God.

Here's where the "not so" part of Paul's statement comes in-to play. Since your darkened understanding, alienation from God, and moral deadness had no part in your learning Christ; they should have no part in how you live once you've learned Christ. Now that you've learned and understood the truth about Jesus and the life God intends for you—a life dedicated to living out His will through obeying His word and serving Him—God expects you to act on that truth by changing.

The first change you need to make is to *put off*, literally to renounce or lay down your sins like taking off an old dirty coat (Ephesians 4:22). The Greek word used for *put off* is in the active tense, which means you are responsible for taking the first step to stop sinning. God won't make the choice for you. Other believers can't make the choice for you. You must decide for yourself to stop sinning. But where do you start?

Paul says you need to start by putting off your "former conduct"—the "old man," which includes the darkened understanding, alienated life, and deadened conscience beliefs and actions you practiced before you were saved and still do. If you don't start working to put off your "old man" sins, Paul says they will "grow corrupt" and "deceive" you. Your "old man" will begin to seduce you away from your new faith and delude you into fulfilling your old sinful desires and appetites.[7] If you don't actively work to put off your old self, the evil that controlled you before you were saved can grow even stronger than it was before.

One way to know which sins to put off is by identifying any you feel bad about. The Bible calls this "godly sorrow" and is a sign that the Holy Spirit is working in your renewed conscience (2 Corinthians 7:10-11). Knowing the difference between the Holy Spirit's conviction and Satan's attack is essential. I remember years ago Martha Miller, my Pastor's wife, said that the Holy Spirit's conviction is always specific, and the Devil's attack is always general. God points at your sin and says, "Change." The Devil points at you and says, "Failure."

But before I talk about putting off sin, you must create the healthy spiritual environment necessary for overcoming sin. You may not know it, but when you receive and believe in Jesus, you begin a lifelong battle between what the Bible calls the flesh and the Spirit. "For the flesh lusts against the Spirit, and the Spirit against the flesh; and these are contrary to one another so that you do not do the things that you wish" (1 Peter 2:11; Galatians 5:17). Your flesh is the "old man" darkened understanding, alienated life, and deadened conscience, beliefs, and actions you practiced before you were saved. The Spirit is the Holy Spirit who makes His home in you when you're saved. Together, they are in a constant battle for control in your life.

One of the most essential spiritual truths you can learn is that you hold the key to who wins the battle between the flesh and the Spirit. Paul explains why in Galatians 6:7–8, where he says, ". . . whatever a man sows, that he will also reap. For he who sows to his flesh will of the flesh reap corruption, but he who sows to the Spirit will of the Spirit reap everlasting life." The more time and energy you invest "sowing" to the Spirit and not "sowing" to your flesh, the more you'll reap the benefits of the life God intends for you.

How do you sow to the Spirit? Paul explains how in Romans 8:5, saying, "For those who live according to the flesh set their minds on the things of the flesh, but those who live according to the Spirit, the things of the Spirit." Simply put, what you set your mind on determines how you live.

There are two ways to "set" your mind on the flesh or the Spirit. The first is through what you choose to put into your mind. Paul says, "The deeds of the flesh are evident, which are adultery, fornication, uncleanness, lewdness, idolatry, sorcery, hatred, contentions, jealousies, outbursts of wrath, selfish ambitions, dissensions, heresies, envy, murder, drunkenness, revelries, and the like" (Galatians 5:19–21).

The more you expose your mind to these fleshly things through the music you listen to, the TV shows and movies you watch, what you read, and what you see on the Internet, the more you feed your flesh. On the other hand, the more you expose your mind to things that include "love, joy, peace, longsuffering, kindness, goodness, faithfulness, gentleness, self-control" (Galatians 5:22–23) through Bible reading, church attendance, Christian music, literature, and programming, the more you will live in the Spirit.

The second way you set your mind on the flesh or the Spirit is through the people you choose to spend time with. In 2 Corinthians 6:14–18, Paul says:

> Do not be unequally yoked together with unbelievers. For what fellowship has righteousness with lawlessness? And what communion has light with darkness? And what accord has Christ with Belial? Or what part has a believer with an unbeliever? And what agreement has the temple of God with idols? For you are the temple of the living God. As God has said:

> "I will dwell in them
> And walk among them.
> I will be their God,
> And they shall be My people."

> Therefore

> "Come out from among them
> And be separate, says the Lord.
> Do not touch what is unclean,
> And I will receive you.
> I will be a Father to you,
> And you shall be My sons and daughters,
> Says the Lord Almighty."

Paul isn't saying you can't associate with unbelievers at all. When he wrote to the Corinthian Christians "not to keep company with sexually immoral people," he said, "Yet I certainly did not mean with the sexually immoral people of this world, or with the covetous, or extortioners, or idolaters, since then you would need to go out of the world" (1 Corinthians 5:9–10). Instead, they were "not to keep company with anyone named a brother, who is sexually immoral, or covetous, or an idolater, or a reviler, or a drunkard, or an extortioner--not even to eat with such a person" (1 Corinthians 5:11). However, Paul does say you should "not be deceived: 'Evil company corrupts good habits'" (1 Corinthians 15:33). The more time you spend with unbelievers and unrepentant Christians and the closer your associations with them, the more they will feed your flesh.

If you limit your time with people who live according to a darkened understanding, alienation from God, and a deadened conscience, whether they're unbelievers are unrepentant Christians, and spend more time with Christians who are walking with Jesus, they will help you set your mind on the Spirit. That's why the writer of Hebrews says to "consider one another in order to stir up love and good works, not forsaking the assembling of ourselves together, as is the manner of some, but exhorting one another, and so much the more as you see the Day approaching" (Hebrews 10:24–25).

There's an old Native American tale that illustrates the battle between the flesh and the Spirit.

> A chief was telling a gathering of young braves about the struggle within us. "It is like two dogs fighting inside of us," the chief told them. "There is one dog who wants to do the right things and the other dog always wants to do the wrong. Sometimes the good dog seems stronger and is winning the fight, but sometimes the bad dog is stronger and wrong is winning the fight."
> "Who is going to win in the end?" a young brave asked.
> The chief answered, "The one you feed."[8]

As a teenager, I experienced firsthand the consequences of feeding the flesh instead of the Spirit. My family stopped going to church soon after I was saved. Several years later, in my early teens, I returned to church and started to live for Christ. At first, I spent all my time with my church friends, but then I decided to spend time with my unsaved friends to try and "influence them for Christ."

I thought I could spend time with them without affecting me, but I was wrong. The more time I spent with my old friends, the weaker my faith became. It wasn't long before I stopped spending time with my saved friends. Eventually, I started doing drugs and swearing like a sailor. I was worse off than before I started living for Christ. My language became so foul that even my unsaved friends wanted nothing to do with me. Fortunately, God used isolation from my unsaved friends to bring me back into the church.

As I wrap up this section on the battle between the flesh and the Spirit, I want to leave you with a promise and a warning. First, God promises that if "you walk in the Spirit," you "shall not fulfill the lust of the flesh" (Galatians 5:16). Second, God warns you about the consequences of your choices to live in the flesh or the Spirit saying, "For to be carnally minded is death, but to be spiritually minded is life and peace" (Romans 8:6).

The point: When you learn Christ, He opens the door to change. The first change you must make is to turn away from your "old man" sins. You determine how successful you are by whether you walk in the spirit or the flesh. If you don't choose to change, you can become more sinful than before you were saved. This is the law of sowing and reaping.

## 3. Learning Christ gives you the power to change

*". . . and be renewed in the spirit of your mind, and that you put on the new man which was created according to God, in true righteousness and holiness." (Ephesians 4:23–24)*

Although change starts when you choose to stop sinning, your decision doesn't give you the power to change. The second part of change happens when God does His part to make you new. Unlike the active word put off, the Greek tense of the word be renewed is passive, which means it's something done to you.

Being renewed happens when God transforms the spirit of your mind, much like what happens when you learn Christ. God renews both your spirit, your immaterial nature, which enables you to communicate with Him, and your mind, the moral consciousness by which you recognize the will of God for your life.[9] God draws you closer to Him by strengthening your conscience and empowering you to do His will. Paul describes this process in Philippians 2:12–13:

> Therefore, my beloved, as you have always obeyed, not as in my presence only, but now much more in my absence, work out your own salvation with fear and trembling; for it is God who works in you both to will and to do for His good pleasure.

When you choose to do your part and stop sinning, God does His part and works on you from the inside to change you on the outside.

The final step toward change happens when you replace your sin with the good things God wants you to do instead. The verb tense of putting on is active, so you must do it. "Putting on the new man" means you've decided to be the new person God wants you to be. It's like putting on new clothes at the beginning of each day. Once you receive and believe in Jesus, you have what it takes to put on the new man because "if anyone is in Christ, he is a new creation; old things have passed away; behold, all things have become new" (2 Corinthians 5:17).

God created your "new man" to have true righteousness that produces words and actions done with integrity and sincerity of heart, living each moment consistent with His commands. He also created your new man in holiness so you can live out your faith spiritually and socially by separating yourself from the world and its worship of lesser things. God created you to be righteous and holy because He wants you to reflect His character.[10]

The point: While change starts with deciding to put off the "old man," change only happens because God works in you and gives you the desire and energy to carry it out. After you put off the old man and God renews your mind, you must put on the new person God created you to be by living out your spiritual life in a way that reflects His moral character.

## Conclusion

After you "learn Christ" through the Gospel, God expects you to live the new life He intends. He expects you to actively participate in His work to transform you into the new person He created you to be by putting off the old, letting Him renew the spirit of your mind, and putting on the new.

You need to stop living like you did before you were saved. You need to change by:

<u>Putting off the old</u>        and        <u>Putting on the new</u>

Discussion Questions:

1. Do you have any thoughts or questions about this chapter?

2. When were you saved?

3. What changed when you got saved?

4. Where have you seen changes in your life between then and now?

5. How are you feeding the flesh? How are you feeding the spirit?

6. Name one area you would like to see change in your life.

# 3

# Put off Lying

*Therefore, putting away lying . . . (Ephesians 4:25)*

## 1. You need to change by putting off lying

*"Therefore, putting away lying . . ." (Ephesians 4:25a)*

Like most boys in the fourth grade, Bobby liked to play with his friends, ride his bike, and build model cars. And like many fourth-grade boys, he had a crush on his teacher, Miss Rogers. Every year at the beginning of fall, Miss Rogers chose a student to help decorate her classroom with a wild assortment of leaves, pumpkins, black cats, and ghosts. To qualify, the student had to have all their class work up to date and complete.

Unfortunately, Bobby was a bit forgetful. It wasn't long into the school year before he fell victim to Miss Rogers' "Lost Box." Any books left out at the end of the day went into the Lost Box and could only be returned after the student paid a dollar. When Miss Rogers announced the opportunity to help her decorate the classroom, Bobby was excited about the chance to spend time with her. The only problem was that he wasn't current on his homework since his workbook was in the Lost Box.

Bobby was faced with a dilemma. He knew he should tell his parents about his carelessness with his workbook and ask them for the dollar he needed to get it back and catch up on all the work he hadn't done in the previous weeks. But he also knew that he could never finish in time to qualify to help Miss Rogers. His cunning nine-year-old mind began to rationalize the situation. He thought, *I was up to date when my workbook was put in the Lost Box, so I could apply to help Miss Rogers.*

Bobby went to Miss Rogers and volunteered to be her helper. When she asked him if his work was up to date and complete, he proudly nodded and said yes. He spent the next few days helping Miss Rogers cut out figures from construction paper and putting up decorations and borders. Bobby felt little tinges of guilt but quickly pushed them aside. Everything was great until another fourth-grade boy with a crush on Miss Rogers noticed Bobby's workbook in the Lost Box. Then came the accusations, the confrontation, and the confession. Bobby was given detention for a week and had to watch someone else finish his work. More importantly, Bobby lost the good relationship he had with Miss Rogers. Like Bobby, you and I learned to lie at an early age.

The first thing Paul says you must put off to be ready for Christ to use is lying. Here are just a few of the things the Bible has to say about lying:

- Lying is one of the first sins the Bible describes. When the serpent lied to Eve about the consequences of eating the fruit from the tree of the knowledge of good and evil, He told her, "You will not surely die" (Genesis 3:4).
- Lying is one of the last sins the Bible names in Revelation 22:15, where John says, "whoever loves and practices a lie" will not be able to enter heaven.
- Proverbs 6:16 says lying lips are one of the seven things God finds detestable.
- The devil is called the father of lies (John 8:38).
- Lying is forbidden in the Ten Commandments (Exodus 20:16).
- The Bible says God never lies since "it is impossible for God to lie" (Hebrews 6:18).

Lying is a great place to start changing after learning Christ because it's a central part of everyday life. People lie about everything, from their taxes to their age and weight. Lying is anything you do that communicates a falsehood or what is false or fictitious.[1]

If you want to stop lying, you must understand why you lie. There are two primary reasons you lie. One is you're afraid to face the consequences of telling the truth. The Bible gives several examples of people who lied to avoid the consequences of telling the truth. Sarah lied when the Lord confronted her for laughing when He told Abraham she would have a baby the same time next year because "she was afraid" (Genesis 18:15). David lied when he was escaping from King Saul and fled to one of the cities of the Philistines. Once he got there, he realized it wasn't a good idea to run to the Philistines for protection because he had killed thousands of Philistines in the war between them and Israel. He pretended to be crazy at the city gates and started foaming at the mouth because he feared the Philistine leaders would kill him (1 Samuel 21:10–15). Peter lied about knowing Jesus while Jesus was on trial because he was afraid he would be arrested, too (Matthew 26:69–75). When I stole the ice cream bar, I lied to my Sunday school teacher because I was afraid she would tell my parents.

The other reason is that you think lying will improve a situation in a way that the truth will not. The Bible also has several examples of people lying because they thought it would improve a situation in a way the truth would not. Ananias and Sapphira lied to Peter when they said they gave all the money from selling a piece of property to the church. However, they only gave part of the money because they wanted men's praise (Acts 5:1–11). Zacchaeus, the tax collector, lied about how much people owed in taxes so he could keep the extra money and become rich (Luke 19:1–8). An Amalekite soldier lied to King David about killing King Saul so he could get a reward (1 Samuel 31:1–6; 2 Samuel 1:1–16). He ended up losing his head instead.

The point: The Bible makes God's feelings about lying very clear. Lying is a sin, and it is detestable to Him. There are two primary reasons you lie: (1) you don't want to face the consequences of telling the truth (fear), and (2) you think lying will improve a situation in a way the truth will not (greed).

## 2. To put off lying, you need to avoid the mistake of the "good lie"

The evil of lying seems clear, given what God's word says about it. However, many Christians today mistakenly believe lying in certain circumstances, like preventing harm, is not wrong. The most common scenario they use to defend this belief is lying to protect Jews in Nazi Germany. The story usually goes like this, "Let's say you live in Nazi Germany, and you have Jews hiding in your living room. The SS guards knock on your door and ask if you're hiding Jews. What do you do?"[2] The people who believe in what I call the "good lie" say that lying in this situation would not be sinning because you're trying to protect someone's life. According to those who believe in the "good lie," lying to save a life isn't sinning. This seems like a reasonable belief, but is it a biblically accurate one?

Many use two passages to justify their belief in the "good lie." The first is Exodus 1. The king of Egypt commanded the Jewish midwives to kill the baby boys so he could control the booming Jewish slave population.

> Then the king of Egypt spoke to the Hebrew mid-
> wives, of whom the name of one was Shiphrah and
> the name of the other Puah; and he said, "When you
> do the duties of a midwife for the Hebrew women,
> and see them on the birthstools, if it is a son, then
> you shall kill him; but if it is a daughter, then she shall
> live." But the midwives feared God, and did not do
> as the king of Egypt commanded them, but saved the
> male children alive. (Exodus 1:15–17)

The midwives refused to obey the king's command and didn't kill the baby boys. When the king learned about it, he asked the midwives why they weren't obeying his command, saying, "Why have you done this thing, and saved the male children alive" (Exodus 1:18)?

This is where the lie comes into play. "The midwives said to Pharaoh, 'Because the Hebrew women are not like the Egyptian women; for they are lively and give birth before the midwives come to them'" (Exodus 1:19). The story ends with God blessing the midwives for their actions and giving them their own families.

> Therefore God dealt well with the midwives, and the people multiplied and grew very mighty. And so it was, because the midwives feared God, that He provided households for them. So Pharaoh commanded all his people, saying, "Every son who is born you shall cast into the river, and every daughter you shall save alive" (Exodus 1:20–22).

Those who believe in the "good lie" argue that God didn't see the lie the midwives told as a sin because He blessed them by giving them families as a reward for lying. But did God bless the midwives for lying to the king, or did He bless them for another reason?

The answer is in the story itself. Verse 17 says, "But the midwives FEARED God, and did not do as the king of Egypt commanded them but, saved the male children alive." Then in verses 20 and 21, Moses says, "Therefore God dealt well with the midwives, and the people multiplied and grew very mighty. And so it was, because the midwives FEARED God, that He provided households for them." According to the passage, God blessed the midwives because they feared Him and disobeyed the king by saving the babies. The passage doesn't say God blessed them for lying.

Another explanation for why the midwives lied can be found in the previous section's reasons for lying. The midwives lied because they feared punishment for disobeying the king's command to kill the baby boys.

The second passage is in Joshua 2. The Jews were camped by the Jordan River and about to invade the land of Canaan. Joshua sent spies to check out Jericho, the first city they would attack. When the spies entered the city, they met a prostitute named Rahab, who welcomed them into her house. The king of Jericho heard the Jews had sent spies and that Rahab had taken in strangers, so he sent soldiers to capture them. The soldiers ordered Rahab to "Bring out the men who have come to you, who have entered your house, for they have come to search out all the country (vs. 3)," but she hid them in a pile of flax on her roof and lied, saying.

> Yes, the men came to me, but I did not know where they were from. And it happened as the gate was being shut, when it was dark, that the men went out. Where the men went I do not know; pursue them quickly, for you may overtake them. vs. 4-5

The soldiers immediately set out on the road back to the Jordan River to capture them. After making the spies promise to save her and her family when they attacked the city, she told them to "Get to the mountain, lest the pursuers meet you. Hide there three days, until the pursuers have returned. Afterward you may go your way (vs. 14)." Then, she let them down a rope out her window, which happened to be on the city wall. The spies did what she said and returned safely to their camp.

The story goes on to tell how God saved Rahab's family when the Jews attacked and how she became the great, great grandmother of King David. Rahab is praised in the Hebrews 11 Hall of Faith and the book of James for her actions.

The "good lie" people argue that Rahab was rewarded for lying to the soldiers. However, as in the case of the midwives, the Bible tells a different story. Hebrews 11:31 says, "By faith the harlot Rahab did not perish with those who did not believe, when she had received the spies with peace." According to the writer of Hebrews, Rahab was rewarded for receiving the spies into her home in peace. James 2:25 says, "Likewise, was not Rahab the harlot also justified by works when she received the messengers [spies] and sent them out another way?" James says Rahab was rewarded for receiving the spies and telling them to go up into the mountains and wait three days before returning to the Jewish camp. Again, none of these passages say Rahab was blessed because she lied. In both the case of the midwives and Rahab, the "good lie" argument is based solely on silence.

You may wonder why God would bless the midwives and Rahab if their lies were sinful. The story of Jacob lying to his father points to the answer. Jacob's father, Isaac, told his oldest son, Esau, to go hunting and prepare a meal for him so he could bless him. Isaac's wife Rebecca overheard the conversation and advised Jacob, their younger son, to deceive his father and steal his brother's blessing, and that's exactly what Jacob did.

Jacob repeatedly lied to his father. He lied when he said he was Esau. He lied about where and how he got the meat, saying, "The Lord your God brought *it* to me" (Genesis 27:20). He deceived his father by putting animal skins on his hands and neck and wearing Esau's clothes. He even lied to his father when asked if he was Esau, boldly claiming, "I *am*" (Genesis 27:24). When Esau found out what happened, he asked his father to take back God's blessing from Jacob and give it to him. Isaac answered, "I have blessed him—and indeed he shall be blessed" (Genesis 27:33).

Almost everyone would agree that Jacob's lies were sinful. But if Jacob's lies were sins, why did God bless him? The Psalmist's answer is in Psalms 103:8–14:

> The Lord is merciful and gracious,
> Slow to anger, and abounding in mercy.
> He will not always strive with us,
> Nor will He keep His anger forever.

He has not dealt with us according to our sins,
Nor punished us according to our iniquities.

For as the heavens are high above the earth,
So great is His mercy toward those who fear Him;
As far as the east is from the west,
So far has He removed our transgressions from us.
As a father pities his children,
So the Lord pities those who fear Him.
For He knows our frame;
He remembers that we are dust.

The message from these biblical accounts is that God blessed the people who lied despite their lies, not because of them. God knows you're only human. He also knows how your human fears and greed can get the better of you. While God doesn't bless you for lying, there are times when He doesn't judge you with immediate earthly consequences. Remember, however, that this isn't always the case. According to Acts 5, when Ananias and Sapphira lied about how much money they sold a piece of land for, God struck them dead for their lie.

Another error of the "good lie" is the mistaken belief that God can't miraculously save people from harm, that if the midwives had told the truth, they and the babies would have died, and if Rahab had told the truth, she and the spies would have died. But there are numerous stories in the Bible where people should have died for doing the right thing and didn't. God miraculously saved people like Joseph, David, Daniel, Shadrach, Meshach and Abednego, Peter, Paul, John, etc., from certain death. We don't know what would have happened if the midwives and Rahab had told the truth. Based on God's miraculous intervention to save other people's lives in the Bible, we know that God could easily have protected them from harm.

But what if you tell the truth and God doesn't save you, and you suffer harm? The next error of the "good lie" is the mistaken belief that God never wants you to suffer harm. Sometimes God expects you to suffer harm at the hands of people who hate Him so you can honor Him. Jesus' disciples faced this choice when the Jewish leaders commanded them to stop telling others about Jesus. They said:

> We ought to obey God rather than men. The God of our fathers raised up Jesus whom you murdered by hanging on a tree. Him God has exalted to His right hand to be Prince and Savior, to give repentance to Israel and forgiveness of sins. And we are His witnesses to these things, and so also is the Holy Spirit whom God has given to those who obey Him (Acts 5:29–32).

After the Jewish leaders beat the disciples, they "departed from the presence of the council, rejoicing that they were counted worthy to suffer shame for His name" (Acts 5:41). The disciples could have lied and avoided the beating by promising to stop telling people about Jesus. But they chose to suffer the abuse directed at God and told the truth. You can only honor God this way if you put aside your fear and put off lying.

Historically, Christians have believed that lying is always a sin. Christian theologian St. Augustine (354–430) believed "lying was always wrong," although he admitted that never lying "would be very difficult to live up to." Thomas Aquinas (1225–1274) thought "all lies were wrong." Eighteenth-century philosopher, Immanuel Kant (1724–1804), believed that lying was "always wrong" because "we should treat each human being as an end in itself, and never as a mere means. Lying to someone is not treating them as an end in themselves, but merely as a means for the liar to get what they want."[3] Only in the last century, with the rise of moral relativism in Western society, has Christianity accepted the theology of the "good lie."

What about the Nazi scenario mentioned at the beginning of this section? What if you lived in Nazi Germany or Nazi-occupied territories and had Jews hiding in your living room, and the Nazi guards knocked on your door and asked if you were hiding Jews? [4] What would you do?

The best answer comes from the testimonies of the people who faced this choice in real life. Books like *Things We Couldn't Say* by Diet Eman and James Schaap and *The Hiding Place* by Corrie Ten Boom and Elizabeth and John Sherrill tell how people risked their lives to save Jews and others during the Nazi occupation of Europe.

In The Hiding Place, Corrie Ten Boom tells the story of the Nazis coming to her sister's house during the German occupation of Holland. The Nazis would go into neighborhoods and conduct lightning searches called "razzia" to round up all the young men between the ages of sixteen and thirty and send them off to Germany to work in the munitions factories. [5] Ten Boom recounts the panic and fear she and her relatives felt when the German soldiers came to her sister's home looking for her young nephews. Not surprisingly, they wrestled with this same question of whether there are times when lying is permissible or if it's always a sin.

> We were chatting in the kitchen with Cocky and Katrien when all at once Peter and his older brother, Bob, raced into the room, their faces white. "Soldiers! Quick! They're two doors down and coming this way!"
>
> They jerked the table back, snatched away the rug, and tugged open the trapdoor. Bob lowered himself first, lying down flat, and Peter tumbled in on top of him. We dropped the door shut, yanked the rug over it, and pulled the table back in place. With trembling hands, Betsie, Cocky, and I threw a long tablecloth over it and started laying five places for tea.

There was a crash in the hall as the front door burst open . . . Two uniformed Germans ran into the kitchen, rifles leveled.

"Stay where you are. Do not move. We heard boots coming up the stairs . . ."

"Where are your men?" the shorter soldier asked Cocky in clumsy, thick-accented Dutch.

"These are my aunts," she said, "and this is my grandfather. My father is at his school and my mother is shopping, and—"

"I didn't ask about the whole tribe!" the man exploded in German. Then in Dutch: "Where are your brothers?"

Cocky stared at him a second, then dropped her eyes. My heart stood still. I knew how Nollie had trained her children—but surely, surely now of all times a lie was permissible!

"Do you have brothers?" the officer asked again.

"Yes," Cocky said softly. "We have three."

"How old are they?"

"Twenty-one, nineteen, and eighteen." . . .

"Where are they now?" . . .

Cocky did not miss a breath.

"Why, they're under the table."

Motioning us all away from it with his gun, the soldier seized a corner of the cloth. At a nod from him, the taller man crouched with his rifle cocked. Then he flung back the cloth.

At last the pent-up tension exploded: Cocky burst into spasms of high hysterical laughter. The soldiers whirled around. Was this girl laughing at them?

"Don't take us for fools!" the short one snarled. Furiously he strode from the room and minutes later the entire squad trooped out—not, un-fortunately, before the silent soldier had spied and pocketed our precious pack of tea.[6]

That night at dinner, Ten Boom recalls how they had "the nearest thing to a bitter argument our close-knit family had ever had."[7] They wrestled with the implications of their choices to lie or tell the truth, both in the sight of God and in the lives of the people they were trying to protect. Some, like Corrie, believed that lying was permissible when it was the only way to protect people from harm. Others, like Cocky, believed that lying was always a sin and that in situations where telling the truth could put people at risk, one needed to trust God with the consequences because He is the one who commands us to tell the truth and not lie. Amazingly, there are nu-merous examples of people doing this very thing.

Deit Eman, in her book *Things We Couldn't Say*, tells the story of a Jewish man and his wife whom German soldiers were herding onto a deportation train that would take them to a concentration camp. A group of fishermen mistakenly tried to board the train, and in the resulting confusion, the Jewish man and his wife slipped away from the soldiers and the line of Jews waiting for deportation. How-ever, they were trapped on the platform because they couldn't get out of the station without a ticket, and the Jews who were being deported weren't given tickets. Instead of lying and making up a story about losing their ticket, they went to the train official guarding the exit and told him they didn't have a ticket. While this should have set off an alarm that would have sent them back to the death train, the "man in the booth took one quick look at him and said, 'Quick—go on'" and let the man and his wife escape.[8]

In another story, Ten Boom's sister, Nollie, had a blonde-haired, blue-eyed Jew named Annaliese living as her housemaid. One day, the Dutch collaborators (the S.D.) came to her home, "pointed to Annaliese and said, 'Is this a Jew?'"[9] Without hesitation, Nollie an-swered, "Yes." They immediately arrested Nollie and sent Annaliese to be processed for deportation to Germany. Everyone, including Ten Boom, thought Nollie was "crazy." However, Nollie sent Ten Boom a message from her jail cell, declaring, "No ill will happen to Annaliese. God will not let them take her to Germany. He will not let her suffer because I obeyed him."[10] Six days later, ten Boom learned that Annaliese and all the Jews with her had been rescued by the resistance and sent to safety.[11] Seven weeks later, Nollie was released from prison "pallid faced, but as radiant as ever."[12] Despite what seemed like an impossible situation, God intervened and delivered them both.

What did people who lived in Nazi-occupied territories and hid Jews in their living rooms do when the SS guards knocked on their door and asked if they were hiding Jews or young Dutch boys? Some, like Corrie Ten Boom, lied and escaped death, while others, like her father, lied and died. Some told the truth and lived, while others told the truth and died. Not surprisingly, only the stories where people told the truth and then saw God's hand at work are described as "providential"[13] and "miraculous."[14] The bottom line is that the Nazi argument is false. Lying didn't guarantee deliverance any more than telling the truth guaranteed death.

Here are a few concluding thoughts about avoiding the mistake of the "good lie." If you're ever faced with the choice of lying to save someone's life or telling the truth, remember that the God who commands you to tell the truth and not lie has the providential and miraculous power to carry out His will and bring glory to His name in the most impossible of situations. On the other hand, you may lie because you feel that the situation warrants it, and God saves you. But that doesn't mean your lie isn't a sin. It only means that God has been merciful and gracious to you and hasn't dealt with you the way your sins deserve because He remembers you are "but dust" (Psalm 103:1–14).

You must also be very careful about calling things "good" that God calls "sin." Isaiah 5:20 warns, "Woe to those who call evil good, and good evil; Who put darkness for light, and light for darkness." If lying is always a sin and you call it good, you risk suffering from God's discipline. On the other hand, if you call lying evil, you can confess it, receive God's forgiveness and restoration, and declare with the Psalmist, "As far as the east is from the west, so far has He removed our transgressions from us" (Psalms 103:12).

Next, I believe lying attacks the heart of what Paul identifies as the mark of a healthy church. Paul says in Ephesians 4:14-16

> That we should no longer be children, tossed to and fro and carried about with every wind of doctrine, by the trickery of men, in the cunning craftiness of deceitful plotting,
>
> *but, speaking the truth in love, may grow up in all things into Him who is the head--Christ--*
>
> from whom the whole body, joined and knit together by what every joint supplies, according to the effective working by which every part does its share, causes growth of the body for the edifying of itself in love. (Emphasis added)

Paul's solution for a childish, immature church is "speaking the truth in love." Paul adds no addenda, exceptions, or conditions to speaking the truth in love. Paul's command is to speak the truth in love, period.

It's possible that someone could argue that "in love" is where the lie fits in, but author Dr. Paul Tripp, in his book *New Morning Mercies: a Daily Gospel Devotional,* beautifully refutes the possibility of this idea.

> Contrary to popular opinion, love and truth don't stand in opposition to one another. In fact, you can't really have one without the other. To love truth, you have to

be committed to love, and to love love, you have to be
committed to truth. The most loving person who ever
lived, so loving that he died a cruel and bloody public
death for crimes that others committed, was at the
same time the most forthright and honest truth speaker
that the world had ever known. It was not just that the
love of Jesus never contradicted his candor and his
candor never inhibited his love. No, there was something more profound going on. His commitment to
truth speaking was propelled by his love. The biblical
call to love will never force you to trim, deny, or bend
the truth, and the biblical call to truth will never ask you
to abandon God's call to love your neighbor…

Truth isn't mean and love isn't dishonest. They are two
sides of the same righteous agenda that longs for the
spiritual welfare of another.[15]

Finally, you may think the "good lie" is a purely hypothetical
issue since most people don't have to face the dilemma of telling the
truth or lying to save someone's life. You would be wrong. Many
who believe in the "good lie" use it for what I call the "greater good."
A follower of the "good lie," I'll call him "GL," complained
on a popular Christian radio program about a Christian Writer, I'll
call him "CW," who wrote an article to raise awareness about the suffering of Palestinians. While writing the article, he included false information about the Jews that painted them negatively. When GL
read the article, he contacted CW about the incorrect information
and asked him to retract his statements. CW refused to change the
story because he believed his story was helping the suffering Palestinians. The problem with using the "good lie" for the "greater good" is
that its application is subjective. Who decides when a lie is for the
"greater good" and when it's not?

When a church accepts the "good lie" for the "greater good" argument, lying becomes an option for dealing with its problems. The harsh reality, however, is that church leaders or members who use lying often use it to hide their mistakes, avoid accountability, or promote their agenda, setting their churches up for catastrophe.

Mars Hill Church in Seattle, Washington, learned this lesson the hard way. Mars Hill had over 13,000 weekly attendees, multiple campuses throughout Seattle, and a worldwide impact. By all appearances, Mars Hill was a thriving church. Then, in 2014 Mars Hill was called out for using deceptive practices to get their lead Pastor, Mark Driscoll's book on the New York Times best-seller list. The church and its leaders probably believed they weren't doing anything wrong, that this was a "good lie" that would benefit people who would never read the book if it wasn't on the best seller list. But when the truth came out, the pastor, leadership, and church were condemned for their actions and lost their credibility. The church of 13,000 members had to close its doors within just a few months. Every church I've seen use lying as a tool for the "greater good" has destroyed itself from within. There is no room for a lie in the truth or the church.

The point: Some Christians have embraced the idea of the "good lie" to justify lying in certain situations, using the good things that happened to some people who lied in the Old Testament as proof. However, the real explanation is that God is merciful and doesn't always give us what we deserve. While lying isn't usually the end of the world, it can have terrible consequences. Believing in the "good lie" may weaken your resolve to stop lying and keep you from making the first change God wants you to make now that you're saved.

## Conclusion

Lying is a basic human condition. You started lying almost as soon as you could communicate, but God wants you to put off lying because it's the old way you used to live. To start putting off lying, you need to understand these three things: lying is wrong, you lie for a reason, and you need to avoid believing in the "good lie."

You need to take the first step to change by:

Putting off the old        and        Putting on the new
Lying

Discussion Questions

1. Do you have any thoughts or questions about this chapter?

2. Why do you lie?

3. How has lying affected your relationships in the past?

4. When has lying gotten you into trouble?

5. To whom could you apologize for lying?

6. What do you think about the "good lie"?

# 4

# Put on Truthfulness

*"Let each one of you speak truth with his neighbor," for we are members of one another (Ephesians 4:25)*

## 1. You need to replace lying with speaking the truth
*"Let each one of you speak truth with his neighbor . . ." (Ephesians 4:25)*

A pastor's job is like most others. Some parts are rewarding; others are frustrating. From an earthly perspective, there aren't a lot of financial advantages to being a Pastor. For most, the pay is just enough to get by. Still, Pastors worldwide faithfully serve God in the church.

Surprisingly, one of the few financial advantages for pastors in the U. S. comes from the federal government. Pastors get to designate a portion of their income as a housing allowance—the actual cost of maintaining a household—that's deducted from their taxable income. This can be a substantial amount and significantly lessen a pastor's tax burden. The tax law clearly states that the Designated Housing Allowance must be made using specific wording, approved by the church's governing body, and recorded before the New Year. I usually do it the first week.

In 2016, I somehow forgot to designate my housing allowance and didn't discover my mistake until the end of April. I immediately completed the process and forgot about it for the rest of the year. When preparing the financial reports for our church's accountant, I realized how much of an impact my mistake would have on my taxes.

I put off doing my report longer than usual, wrestling with what I should do. I searched for some loophole to ease my conscience about claiming the total housing expenses for the year. But according to our church tax guide, the designation only applied to money earned after the designation date. I was left with a choice. I could lie and create a false record showing I had designated my housing allowance in January, or I could tell the truth and deal with the consequences of my mistake. No one would know I falsified the designation unless I was audited, which seemed highly unlikely. The problem was I would know. I told the truth and sent the accountant the correct information.

As I braced myself for filing my taxes, the experience reminded me of how important it is to speak the truth. When Paul says, "Let each one of you speak truth with his neighbor," he's quoting from Zechariah 8:16, where God told the children of Israel how He expected them to live when He brought them back into the Promised Land. God's first command for the returning Israelites was to speak truth to their neighbors.

God's passion for speaking the truth should come as no surprise since truthfulness is central to His character. When God offers His wisdom to whoever will listen in Proverbs 8:7–9, He says:

> "For my mouth will speak truth;
> Wickedness is an abomination to my lips.
> All the words of my mouth are with righteousness;
> Nothing crooked or perverse is in them.
> They are all plain to him who understands,
> And right to those who find knowledge."

According to Solomon, God cares about whether you speak the truth or not, saying:

> He who speaks truth declares righteousness,
> But a false witness, deceit . . .
> The truthful lip shall be established forever,
> But a lying tongue is but for a moment . . .

Lying lips are an abomination to the Lord,
But those who deal truthfully are His delight (Proverbs 12:17, 19, 22).

David said, "Who may abide in Your tabernacle? Who may dwell in Your holy hill? He who walks uprightly, and works righteousness, and speaks the truth in his heart" (Psalms 15:1–2). God wants you to speak the truth!

The word Paul uses for the truth you're to speak is the same Greek word he uses to describe the truth that's in Jesus, which is the reality clearly observed, free from all error or falsehood, and the spiritual truth found only in Him.[1] Paul used both parts of truth when he witnessed to Festus:

> . . . Festus said with a loud voice, "Paul, you are beside yourself! Much learning is driving you mad!" But he said, "I am not mad, most noble Festus, but speak the words of truth and reason. For the king, before whom I also speak freely, knows these things; for I am convinced that none of these things escapes his attention, since this thing was not done in a corner." (Acts 26:24–26)

When Paul says you should speak truth to your neighbor, he uses the Greek word for *speak* which means "to talk at random." Paul's command to speak the truth isn't just for special occasions like swearing oaths or giving testimonies. It's for every part of every conversation you have. The neighbor you're supposed to speak the truth to can be a friend, a fellow Christian, or a total stranger, like in the story Jesus told about the Good Samaritan in Luke 10:25–37. God wants you to speak the truth everywhere to everyone all the time.

I wish I could start this paragraph with, "Speaking the truth is easy!" But it's not. Speaking the reality clearly observed takes courage and wisdom to know what and when to say something and when not to say anything. To speak the truth found in Jesus with someone who wants to understand God's Word or get advice on how to live, you need to study the Bible and "Be diligent to present yourself approved to God, a worker who does not need to be ashamed, rightly dividing the word of truth" (2 Timothy 2:15).

The point: Whether using words or actions, you should be as committed to speaking the truth as you are to God, whose every word is truth, and to Jesus, who is the truth. Being a truth speaker takes hard work and courage. God's plan is for you to speak the truth about the reality clearly observed and the spiritual truth found in Jesus to everyone everywhere, all the time.

## 2. You need to speak the truth in love

While speaking the reality clearly observed and the spiritual truth found in Jesus and His Word is essential, Paul also says you need to speak the truth "in love" so you can help everyone in the church "grow up in all things into Him who is the head—Christ" (Ephesians 4:15). When Paul defined love in 1 Corinthians 13:4 he started by saying "Love suffers long (is patient) and kind." Patience is waiting a long time before you blow up, [2] and kindness is using the most benevolent way possible while upholding moral goodness.[3] You must be patient and kind to speak the truth in love.

Sometimes speaking the truth in love means speaking against evil (2 Corinthians 12: 14–21; see 19–21). It can be hard to tell people about the sin you see in their lives because you don't want to hurt them. However, God often uses others to open our eyes to sin we can't see ourselves. When you bravely speak out against evil in a patient and kind way, God can use you to bring deliverance to the people around you.

Occasionally speaking the truth in love means speaking with sharpness. The word sharpness means to cut off, sometimes severely or abruptly.[4] Paul warned the Corinthian church in 2 Corinthians 13:10, saying, "Therefore I write these things being absent, lest being present I should use sharpness, according to the authority which the

Lord has given me for edification and not for destruction." He also told Titus to rebuke the Cretans "sharply, that they may be sound in the faith, not giving heed to Jewish fables and commandments of men who turn from the truth" (Titus 1:13).

Paul shared a story about when he needed to use sharpness to confront the Apostle Peter. In Acts 10 and 11, God told the Apostle Peter not to "call unclean what God has called clean," including Gentiles—non-Jews. Unfortunately, Peter forgot this lesson when he visited the Christians in the Gentile city of Antioch, and Paul had to confront him publicly.

> Now when Peter had come to Antioch, I withstood him to his face, because he was to be blamed; for before certain men came from James, he would eat with the Gentiles; but when they came, he withdrew and separated himself, fearing those who were of the circumcision. And the rest of the Jews also played the hypocrite with him, so that even Barnabas was carried away with their hypocrisy. But when I saw that they were not straightforward about the truth of the gospel, I said to Peter before them all, "If you, being a Jew, live in the manner of Gentiles and not as the Jews, why do you compel Gentiles to live as Jews?" (Galatians 2:11–14)

Sharpness can be patient when used with controlled intensity instead of the uncontrolled anger associated with blowing up at someone. Sharpness can be kind when used to gain the attention of people engaged in unruly behavior and not punish them. While you should be willing to use sharpness, you shouldn't make sharpness a common practice. If you use sharpness, remember what Paul told the Corinthian believers in 2 Corinthians 10:7–11, that his sharp words are "for edification and not for your destruction." According to Dr. Paul Tripp,

Truth not spoken in love ceases to be truth because it gets bent and twisted by other human agendas, and love that abandons the truth ceases to be love because it forsakes what is best for the person when it has been corrupted by other motives.

Today you are called to loving honesty and honest love. You will be tempted to let one or the others slip from your hands. Pray for the help of the One who remained fully committed to both, even to death. His grace is your only hope of staying true to his righteous agenda. [5]

The Point: You need to speak the truth in love so you can help other Christians "grow up in all things into Him who is the head—Christ" (Ephesians 4:15). To speak the truth in love, you need to speak the reality observed and the spiritual truth found in Jesus with patience and kindness. Speaking the truth in love may require you to speak against evil and occasionally speak with sharpness.

## 3. You have a responsibility to speak truth to the body of Christ

*"For we are members of one another." (Ephesians 4:25)*

Beyond the general command to speak truth to your neighbor, Paul adds another dimension saying, "For we are members of one another." The word "members" means a limb or part of a body and refers to becoming part of the body of Christ—the church—when you put your faith in Jesus.[6] When you become part of the Body of Christ, you also become "individually members of one another" and have a responsibility to help care for each other. (Romans 12:5)

God identifies several ways you need to be truthful and fulfill your responsibility to other Christians, even when it's hard. God expects you to be honest about your offenses when you hurt someone so you can offer healing through an apology. Jesus said in Matthew 5:23–24:

> Therefore if you bring your gift to the altar, and there remember that your brother has something against you, leave your gift there before the altar, and go your way. First be reconciled to your brother, and then come and offer your gift.

I can get angry when I drive, especially when I'm in a hurry. Sometimes my anger is so intense that I say things I shouldn't. On one trip, I yelled at the people in front of me because they were driving slowly, and I was late for an appointment.

Fortunately, the people I yelled at didn't hear me. However, my wife was in the car and listened to every word. She was hurt by what I'd said and told me so. I could have lied to my wife about what I'd done and denied responsibility for hurting her. But God wanted me to be honest about my offense so I could offer her a sincere apology and He could heal her of the injury I caused. I decided to speak the truth and apologized. God expects you to be honest when you offend people and apologize for hurting them.

God also expects you to tell other Christians about the sins you're struggling with so they can pray for you. James 5:16 says, "Confess *your* trespasses to one another and pray for one another, that you may be healed. The effective, fervent prayer of a righteous man avails much." If you're struggling with a particular sin and can't get victory over it, God's solution is to confide in another Christian who can pray for you and hold you accountable.

On the other hand, you may think you should take the offenses committed against you in silence and never tell people when they hurt you. The Bible teaches there are times you should overlook an offense (Proverbs 19:11), but it also teaches there are times you should tell people when they hurt you (Matthew 18:15). That's because—along with using a person's conscience to reveal sin—

sometimes God wants to use you to correct a person to help them get victory over their sin. People are often clueless about their sins until someone like you tells them that what they're doing hurts others. Sometimes God wants you to speak about your hurt to the person who sins against you so He can deal with their sin and make them more like Christ (see also James 5:19–20 and Galatians 6:1–2).

Next, God expects you to be honest with the people who have authority over you. Peter said in 1 Peter 2:13–17:

> Therefore submit yourselves to every ordinance of man for the Lord's sake, whether to the king as supreme, or to governors, as to those who are sent by him for the punishment of evildoers and for the praise of those who do good. For this is the will of God, that by doing good you may put to silence the ignorance of foolish men—as free, yet not using liberty as a cloak for vice, but as bondservants of God. Honor all people. Love the brotherhood. Fear God. Honor the king.

Most would agree that lying to get something the Bible says you shouldn't have, or to do something you shouldn't is choosing to walk away from the life God intends you to live. But God also uses authorities He puts over you to guide you in ways His Word doesn't. The Bible may not say, "You shall not marry Brad," but God can use your parents to tell you that you shouldn't marry Brad. If you lie to an authority like your parents (Ephesians 6:1-3), employer (Ephesians 6:5-8), or government (1 Peter 2:13–17) to do or get what you want, you risk living the life of death you had before you were saved instead of the life God intends for you to live now.

Finally, God expects you to be honest about your faith in Christ in the face of hostility. Peter said in 1 Peter 3:13–17:

And who *is* he who will harm you if you become followers of what is good? But even if you should suffer for righteousness' sake, *you are* blessed. *"And do not be afraid of their threats, nor be troubled."* But sanctify the Lord God in your hearts, and always *be* ready to *give* a defense to everyone who asks you a reason for the hope that is in you, with meekness and fear; having a good conscience, that when they defame you as evildoers, those who revile your good conduct in Christ may be ashamed. For *it is* better, if it is the will of God, to suffer for doing good than for doing evil.

Sometimes Christians are faced with something the Bible calls "persecution." Persecution happens when a non-believer who hates God attacks a believer because of their love for God. Jesus explained why people do this when He said, "'A servant is not greater than his master.' If they persecuted me, they will also persecute you" (John 15:20). Christians worldwide are attacked because they believe in Jesus and love and honor God. During the Boxer Rebellion of 1900, students at a Christian school in China were persecuted because of their faith. Chinese soldiers put a cross on the ground and told the students to deny their faith by stepping on the cross, or they would be killed. Several students stepped on the cross, but a young girl refused and walked around the cross. She was killed. Afterward, every other student walked around the cross and gave their lives to honor God.[7] They could have lied about their faith and walked on the cross to save themselves, but sometimes, as we discussed in the previous chapter about the "good lie," God expects you to suffer at the hands of people who hate Him so you can honor Him. Jesus told His disciples in Matthew 5:11-16,

> Blessed are you when they revile and persecute you, and say all kinds of evil against you falsely for My sake. Rejoice and be exceedingly glad, for great *is* your

reward in heaven, for so they persecuted the prophets who were before you. You are the salt of the earth; but if the salt loses its flavor, how shall it be seasoned? It is then good for nothing but to be thrown out and trampled underfoot by men. You are the light of the world. A city that is set on a hill cannot be hidden. Nor do they light a lamp and put it under a basket, but on a lampstand, and it gives light to all *who are* in the house. Let your light so shine before men, that they may see your good works and glorify your Father in heaven.

You can't be blessed for being salt, light, and a city on a hill if you lie about your faith in Jesus.

The point: God expects you to be truthful when communicating with others in the church because He expects you to fulfill your responsibility to each other as members of the Body of Christ.

## Conclusion

God wants you to stop using your words for selfish purposes and start using them for His righteous purposes. You need to stop lying and practice truthfulness instead.

God wants you to put off the old way of lying and put on the new way of truthfulness.

You need to change by:

Putting off the old    and    Putting on the new
Lying                    Truth

Discussion Questions

1. Do you have any thoughts or questions about this chapter?

2. Why is it hard to tell the truth sometimes?

3. How would telling the truth affect your relationships?

4. When has telling the truth gotten you into trouble?

5. What positive results have you had because you told the truth to authorities?

6. To whom could you bring healing through a sincere apology?

# 5

# Put off Sinning in Your Anger

*"Be angry, and do not sin . . ." (Ephesians 4:26)*

## 1. To avoid sinning in your anger, you must understand the theology of anger

*"Be angry, and do not sin . . ." (Ephesians 4:26)*

It was soon after breakfast that Debbie started feeling a bit off. When her kids, Michael and Jessica, decided to paint a mural on the hallway wall with tempera paint, Debbie reacted with unusual harshness by yelling at the kids and sending them to their rooms. Over the next few hours, Debbie's anger grew.

When her husband Jim came home from work, Debbie was waiting for him at the door. With her hands on her hips, Debbie said, "I've had enough of dealing with these kids. It's your turn to take care of them. I need a break." Jim, a bit surprised by the greeting, asked what had happened. "*Your* kids painted all over the wall!" Jim went into the hall and saw the partially finished mural. On closer inspection, Jim noticed that the paint would wash off easily. He went back to the living room where Debbie was waiting. "Well?" she asked. Jim said he understood why she was upset and then tried to explain that the paint should wash off without much trouble. Debbie exploded, "I can't believe it. You're siding with the kids over me. I could just kill you!" and stormed into the bedroom.

To say Jim was shocked would be an understatement. Jim and Debbie never talked to each other that way. Jim's thoughts quickly went from shock to concern. He was sure something was wrong. It took twenty minutes to convince Debbie to unlock the bedroom door.

Jim sat beside her and said, "Debbie, I know you're upset, but I'm concerned that something else is happening. How do you feel?" When she gave him a vague answer, he touched her forehead. She was burning up. After a call to his in-laws to watch the kids, Jim took Debbie to the clinic. The doctor told Debbie she had a double ear infection. After a few days on an antibiotic, she felt better but was mortified by how she'd treated Jim and the kids.

While you may not have the same anger issues Debbie has when she's sick, you still must deal with anger as a fallen human being in a fallen world. That's why the next thing you need to put off to be ready for Christ to use is the inappropriate use of your anger.

Most words translated as "anger" in the New Testament come from two Greek words, *orgidzo* and *orgay*. These words have a similar root, but they have very different meanings. The Greek word *orgidzo* is a verb meaning "to be provoked to anger, be angry" and is the emotion you experience when you're offended.[1] The Greek word *orgay*, is a noun used to describe "anger exhibited in punishment, hence used for punishment itself."[2] Unfortunately, our English translations aren't consistent in translating these words, so for the sake of clarity, I'll use the word "anger" to translate *orgidzo* (emotions) and the word "wrath" (punishment) to translate *orgay*.

The Bible says God feels the emotion of anger. We know God feels anger because of the parable Jesus told in Matthew 18:21–35. In this parable, God (the king) forgives his servant an enormous debt, but then discovers that the servant he forgave wouldn't forgive a small debt owed to him by someone else. God was "angry" and turned the unforgiving servant over to the torturers until he paid back everything he owed. (Matthew 18:34). God's response to the servant's sin of unforgiveness was to feel anger at the injustice done to one of His subjects.

People also feel anger. Although there are Christians who teach anger is wrong, Paul says anger is an acceptable emotion in Ephesians 4:26, where he says, "Be angry, and do not sin . . ." Dr.

Gary Chapman, in his book *The Other Side of Love: Handling Anger in a Godly Way*, describes the emotion of anger as:

> A strong passion or emotion of displeasure, and usually antagonism, excited by a sense of injury or insult. Anger involves the emotions, the body, the mind, and the will, all of which are stimulated by some event in the individual's life. Anger is always stimulated by an event. It is the emotion that arises when we encounter what we perceive to be wrong . . . when we encounter injustice.[3]

Depending on how strong your emotions are when you feel anger, you might describe yourself as upset, hurt, disappointed, grumpy, irritated, frustrated, angry, furious, etc. These different levels of emotion all express anger.

How do you describe yourself when you get angry?

_____

_____

_____

According to Dr. David Seamands, anger is more than just an emotional response to an injury or offense. "Anger is a divinely implanted emotion . . . designed to be used for constructive spiritual purposes."[4] Anger helps you know when you've been offended so you can properly deal with an offense. An offense is a real action done by someone that hurts someone else.

When you're lied to or treated rudely, anger serves the same purpose in your spirit as pain receptors in your skin. When fire injures your skin, your pain receptors tell your brain that you must protect yourself. In the same way, when an offense like a lie is commit-

64

ted against you, anger lets you know you've been offended so you can take steps to protect yourself from further harm.

Wrath, on the other hand, is different from the emotion of anger. Wrath is the right to demand repayment for an offense. [5] Although it may be hard to understand, God has the right to repay or punish sin. Many accounts in the Bible give details about God punishing sin. One example is in 2 Samuel 6 when King David was trying to move the Ark of God to Jerusalem. God commanded the Jews to carry the Ark with poles (Numbers 4:1–16), but David didn't follow God's instructions. He decided to put the Ark on a cart pulled by oxen instead.

> And when they came to Nachon's threshing floor, Uzzah put out *his hand* to the ark of God and took hold of it, for the oxen stumbled. Then the anger of the Lord was aroused against Uzzah, and God struck him there for *his* error; and he died there by the ark of God. (2 Samuel 6:6–7).

Why would God do this?

Look at what God says about Himself in Jeremiah 17:10, "I, the Lord, search the heart, *I* test the mind, Even to give every man according to his ways, According to the fruit of his doings." While we don't know all the details of David and Uzzah's actions—whether their decisions were based on rebellion or ignorance—we know God was justified in what He did because He knew Uzzah's heart and mind. His knowledge gave Him the right to put Uzzah to death. Although God's wrath is often tempered by His mercy (Isaiah 54:8), He has the right to demand payment for an injustice or offense. That's why we refer to God's wrath as righteous anger. God's wrath is always justified.

Surprisingly, the Bible never positively uses the word "wrath" about people. Paul commands you to let wrath "be put away" from you (Ephesians 4:31). James explains why you can't use wrath to punish others when he says, "So then, my beloved brethren, let every man be swift to hear, slow to speak, slow to wrath; for the wrath of man does not produce the righteousness of God" (James 1:19–20).

You can't use wrath to punish people because you don't have God's righteous qualities described in Jeremiah 17:10. You can't search the heart or test the mind of the person who offends you. You can't even know what punishment would be appropriate for each offense. Anything you do to punish others is wrong. You don't have the right to punish.

---

When have you gotten angry with someone because you made an assumption about their thoughts, feelings, or motives?

_____

_____

_____

_____

---

The point: God and humans feel angry when someone commits an offense against them. The levels of emotion may vary with different offenses, but it's still the same emotion of *orgidzo* anger. The purpose of *orgidzo* anger is to let you know an offense has been committed so you can deal with it properly. Since God can rightly evaluate, judge, and punish offenses, God's righteous wrath is always an appropriate response to sin. However, people can't rightly evaluate, judge, and punish offenses, so a person's wrath is always an inappropriate response to an offense.

## 2. To avoid sinning in your anger, you need to recognize the presence of anger

*"Be angry, and do not sin . . ." (Ephesians 4:26)*

One way to avoid sinning in your anger is to be aware of the emotion of anger. You may have a hard time recognizing your anger for various reasons. Most of us react emotionally when someone says or does something offensive, but when you're raised in a home where anger isn't acknowledged or allowed, you may learn to deny the emotion of anger. While you may have grown up in a home where anger isn't acknowledged or allowed, you probably still experience the "displeasure, and... antagonism excited by a sense of injury or insult."[6] You've just been trained to deny the presence of the emotion of anger.

The key to overcoming the unhealthy practice of denying your anger is transforming how you think about it. Put off the lie that the emotion you're experiencing isn't anger and put on the truth that anger is a good God-given emotion with a purpose. Let God change how you think about anger by memorizing Ephesians 4:26: "Be angry, and do not sin." Accept what godly people say about anger, that "Anger is a divinely implanted emotion... designed to be used for constructive spiritual purposes,"[7] and "is the emotion that arises when we encounter what we perceive to be [a] wrong . . . [or] when we encounter [an] injustice.[8] Ask God to help you recognize when you're experiencing displeasure or feeling antagonized. Trust God that the emotion of anger you feel is good, and accept its presence.

On the other hand, you may have a hard time feeling anger if you grew up in a volatile home where mental illness or addictions created an emotional minefield. When you grow up in this kind of home, you often learn to suppress or "stuff" your emotions to cope with the unhealthy and often chaotic behavior of the mentally ill or addicted person. Unfortunately, just as a person who is less sensitive to pain is in danger of a more severe injury, when you "stuff" your anger, there's a danger of suffering greater emotional and spiritual harm.

The key to overcoming the unhealthy practice of suppressing or stuffing your anger is transforming how you think about it. Put off the lie that emotions like anger are dangerous and put on the truth that your emotions are good and God gave them to you for a reason. Allow God to change how you think about your emotions by memorizing Mark 12:30 which says, "And you shall love the Lord your God with all your heart [including emotions], with all your soul, with all your mind, and with all your strength."

Ask God to help you become aware of your emotions, including anger. While working to become more aware of my emotions, I would stop and reflect when I knew I should be feeling an emotion but wasn't. Then I would figure out what the emotion should be—whether it was happiness or sadness, or grief or anger—and search deep in my heart to find it. Once I found the emotion, I worked at feeling it. The change took time, but eventually, I began to feel my emotions without searching for them. With God's help, this process of emotional reflection can help you learn how to feel your emotions, including anger.

Another thing that can keep you from feeling the emotion of anger is replacing anger with wrath. This problem often comes from growing up in a home where wrath was the typical response to offenses. Wrath can completely overwhelm the feeling of anger.

To overcome the unhealthy practice of replacing anger with wrath, you must put off the lie that the emotion of anger is the same as the wrath you use to punish the person who offends you. Put on the truth that anger's purpose isn't to punish the person who offends you but to let you know you've been offended. Allow God to renew your mind by memorizing the first part of Ephesians 4:26, "Be angry and do not sin," and James 1:19–20, "So then, my beloved brethren, let every man be swift to hear, slow to speak, slow to wrath; for the wrath of man does not produce the righteousness of God."

Meditate on these Scriptures, asking God to help you recognize the difference between "displeasure, and… antagonism, excited by a sense of injury or insult," and the urge to punish the person who offends you.[9] These verses will remind you that the emotion of anger is positive, that you need to take responsibility for your actions, and that you must fight the urge to take vengeance. If you struggle with

68

wrath, take extra steps to ensure the safety and well-being of the people around you by asking a mature brother or sister in Christ to hold you accountable.

The point: To avoid sinning in your anger, you need to be able to feel it. Your ability to feel anger is often determined by the home you grew up in. If you grew up in a home where anger was used correctly, you'll probably recognize it most of the time. If you grew up in a home where anger wasn't allowed, where relational chaos forced you to stuff your emotions, or where the emotion of anger was replaced by wrath, you'll probably struggle to feel it. Feeling anger is essential because you need to be able to feel the emotion of anger to keep from sinning. You can learn to feel your anger through prayer, Bible memorization, and practice.

### 3. To avoid sinning in your anger, you need to learn the difference between justified and unjustified anger
*"Be angry, and do not sin . . ." (Ephesians 4:26)*

While anger helps you know an offense has been committed, it's not always tied to a real offense. Jesus warns about unjustified anger in Matthew 5:22, where He says, "But I say to you that whoever is angry with his brother without a cause shall be in danger of the judgment." Dr. Gary Chapman says your anger can take on two characteristics:

- *Definitive anger [justified]*: anger that has been stimulated by genuine wrongdoing or "Evil."[10]
- *Distorted anger [unjustified]*: anger triggered by a mere disappointment, an unfulfilled desire, a frustrated effort, or any number of things that have nothing to do with any moral transgression. The situation simply has made life inconvenient for us, touched one of our emotional hot spots, or happened at a time when we were emotionally tired or stressed.[11]

Sometimes it's hard to tell if anger is justified or not. Is your anger justified when someone doesn't respond to a hello? Is it justified when you come home after a hard day's work and the chores haven't been done? Is your anger justified when your spouse forgets an important day? Maybe, but you are responsible for making sure your anger is justified because God holds you accountable for how you act when you're angry. Proverbs 3:30 says, "Do not strive with a man without cause, if he has done you no harm." Take time to investigate a situation before you respond to it. God says in Proverbs 18:13, "He who answers a matter before he hears *it,* It *is* folly and shame to him."

The person you say hello to may be distracted by a significant problem they're facing. The chores may not be done because of an emergency. Your spouse may have forgotten about that special day because of an illness or crisis. You must go the extra mile to ensure your emotions are based on truth, not assumptions.

---

Can you think of any recent examples of when you had unjustified anger?

_____

_____

_____

_____

_____

---

Tip: There are physical factors that can disconnect your anger response from an actual offense. Being tired, hungry, sick, stressed, or taking some medications can make you more likely to feel the emotion of anger even though a real offense hasn't been committed. You need to take whatever steps you can to guard against those circumstances to protect yourself and the people around you from unjustified anger.

The point: Anger is a good thing but it isn't perfect. You can experience justified anger tied to a real offense, or you can experience unjustified anger that isn't connected to an offense at all. Since the emotions are the same, you need to investigate the offense to determine if your anger is justified.

## Conclusion

God wants you to put away your old way of sinning in your anger because it only brings death. The new way of using anger is to experience it without sinning. You can use anger without sinning when you understand the theology of anger, recognize the presence of the emotion of anger, and identify the source of your anger to see whether it's justified or unjustified.

God wants you to change by:

<u>Putting off the old</u>    and    <u>Putting on the new</u>
     Abusing Anger

Discussion Questions

1. Do you have any thoughts or questions about this chapter?

2. How did your family express anger when you were growing up?

3. What makes you angry?

4. Where do you struggle most in your anger: using it to punish people, feeling it, or not taking the time to make sure it is justified before you act?

5. When have you had unjustified anger toward someone?

6. To Whom could you apologize for sinning in your anger?

# 6

# Put on Using Anger Properly

*". . . do not let the sun go down on your wrath, nor give place to the devil."*
*(Ephesians 4:26–27)*

## 1. You need to deal with your anger in a timely manner

*". . . do not let the sun go down on your wrath, nor give place to the devil."*
*(Ephesians 4:26–27)*

When Rick invited Bret to a men's breakfast at Eastside Baptist, he started attending the church. He liked working on cars, so he jumped at the opportunity when Rick asked him to help Eastside's Auto Repair Ministry. Bret enjoyed it so much that he signed up as a regular volunteer. A few days later Bret started having stomach pains. He spent the next two months going back and forth to the emergency room, and after several trips to different specialists, he still had no idea what was wrong. Finally, on his last trip to the emergency room, the doctor suggested a HIDA scan to check his gallbladder. The test showed his gallbladder had stopped working, and they took it out the next day. Bret spent the next six weeks recovering.

When Bret finally started feeling better, Rick invited him to the annual Auto Repair Ministry dinner. As Bret was getting his food, Carl, another member of the Repair Ministry team, came up and said, "Hey, freeloader. After missing the whole season, most guys wouldn't have the guts to show their face at an appreciation dinner."

Bret tried to explain what happened, but Carl laughed and said, "Whatever," and then walked away. Bret sat down and ate his food in silence. When the dinner ended, he thanked Rick for inviting him and left. He liked Eastside, but this was more than he could handle. He decided to try another church.

Understanding, recognizing, and identifying your anger is important, but these are only the first steps in learning how to avoid sinning in your anger. The next step is to learn how to deal with it properly.

Paul explains how you should deal with your anger in Ephesians 4:26–27 when he says, "Do not let the sun go down on your wrath, nor give place to the devil." This is an unusual passage about anger because the word translated as "wrath," used only here in the Bible, isn't *orgay* (wrath) or *orgidzo* (anger). It's the word *parorgismós*, which means "the exasperation or anger to which one is provoked,"[1] or the anger you feel because of an offense.

Paul starts by warning you not to "let the sun go down on" the anger you feel because of an offense. He uses sundown as the deadline because the Bible marks sunset as the end of the day. If you don't deal with your anger in a timely manner, by the end of the day, Paul says you "give place to the devil" (Ephesians 4:27). What does it mean to "give place to the devil"?

When you hear the word "give," you might think of giving something to someone, like a piece of gum, but it can also refer to a legal transfer.[2] Jesus used the word "give" this way when He taught about divorce in the Sermon on the Mount. Jesus was comparing the day's religious teachings with what God had in mind. One of those teachings had to do with divorce. Jesus said:

> Furthermore it has been said, "Whoever divorces his wife, let him *give* her a certificate of divorce." But I say to you that whoever divorces his wife for any reason except sexual immorality causes her to commit adultery; and whoever marries a woman who is divorced commits adultery (Matthew 5:31–32, emphasis added).

The Jews had twisted Moses' teachings allowing divorce for certain situations into a license for divorce for any reason (Deuteronomy 24:1). Jesus taught that God only permitted divorce when one spouse cheated on the other. Even then, the divorce wasn't legal until the certificate of divorce was physically placed into the hand of the spouse.[3] The word "give" in Ephesians 4:26 has the same idea of a legal transfer. When you let the sun go down on your wrath, you make a legal transfer to the Devil.

When you think of "place," you might think of a physical location, like your house or a store, but "place" can also have another meaning. In John 11:45–48, the Pharisees struggled with Jesus and His teachings and what they should do about Him. While discussing the problem, they asked, "What shall we do? For this Man works many signs. If we let Him alone like this, everyone will believe in Him, and the Romans will come and take away both our *place* and nation" (emphasis added).

When the Pharisees said they'd lose their "place," they weren't talking about their houses or parking spaces. They were talking about their authority, the role they occupied as rulers.[4] The word "place" in Ephesians 4:26 has the same idea of a position of authority.

Now, apply these meanings of the words "give" and "place" to Ephesians 4:27. When you let the sun go down on the anger you feel because of an offense, you make a legal transfer that gives the devil a position of authority in your life. How does Satan's position of authority work?

An old cartoon version of Gulliver's Travels illustrates this well. After Gulliver was shipwrecked, he washed up on the island of the Lilliputians, people smaller than his little toe. While he lay unconscious on the beach, they tied him down with their tiny ropes. They worked all night, putting on as many cords as possible before he awoke.

When Gulliver woke up, he was held down by hundreds of tiny ropes. None of the ropes alone could have held him, but together they bound him to the ground. The anger you don't deal with— that you let the sun go down on—becomes a tiny rope Satan can use to bind you. The more unresolved anger you have, the more authority you give Satan to bind you up in your Christian walk. What does the devil's position of authority in your life allow him to do?

Suppose the devil's position of authority only gives him the right to bind you from putting off and putting on the things in Ephesians 4:17–32. In that case, it still includes everything from your ability to stop lying and stealing to mastering the more complicated issues of kindness and forgiveness.

---

What sins have you had a hard time getting victory over in your life?

_____

_____

_____

---

The point: If you don't deal with the offenses that cause you anger in a timely manner, you make a legal transaction that gives the devil the position of authority to keep you from growing spiritually and getting victory over sin.

## 2. You need to deal with your anger in a "legal" manner
... *give place* ... *(Ephesians 4:27)*

To avoid sinning in your anger, you need to deal with it in a timely manner, but how are you supposed to deal with "the exasperation or anger to which [you are] provoked?"[5] Fortunately, Paul talks about this same kind of transaction in Romans 12:18–19. Paul says, "If it is possible, as much as depends on you, live peaceably with all men" (Romans 12:18). Ideally, when someone offends you, you should go and confront the person. Then, when the person who offended you sincerely apologizes, you offer forgiveness by saying, "I forgive you."

Unfortunately, things don't always turn out that way. Sometimes you can't or shouldn't confront the person who offended you, or you do confront the person and aren't given a sincere apology. That's why Paul says, "Beloved, do not avenge yourselves, but *rather* give place to wrath; for it is written, '*Vengeance is Mine, I will repay,*' says the Lord" (Romans 12:19). Paul reminds you not to punish the person saying, "do not avenge yourselves" because wrath is never acceptable for you to use. Then Paul gives you a choice to "give place" to wrath instead. This verse is similar to what Paul says in Ephesians 4:26–27. Looking at these two passages together, you can see their parallel structure. Look at Ephesians 4:26-27 and Romans 12:19 side by side. Both passages discuss how to deal with an offense properly and the danger of misusing anger. They both use the words "give" and "place" to deal with anger.

| | |
|---|---|
| *"Be angry, and do not sin":* do not let the sun go down on your wrath (*parorgismós*), | Beloved, do not avenge yourselves, but rather give (*didomi*) place (*topos*) to wrath (*orgay*); |
| nor give (*didomi*) place (*topos*) to the devil. | for it is written, "Vengeance is Mine, I will repay," says the Lord. |
| Ephesians 4:26–27 | Romans 12:19 |

In Ephesians 4:26–27, you "give" a "place," or position of authority to the devil by letting the sun go down on your anger from an offense. However, in Romans 12:18-19, Paul says you can "give" the position of authority to "wrath." Since you've already learned that God is the only one with the right to use wrath, this can only refer to God's wrath. When you're unable to deal with an offense "peaceably," you can make a "legal transfer" that gives God the "position of authority" to deal with the offense on your behalf.

The Bible has several examples of people giving God the "position of authority" to deal with an offense. Nehemiah decided to "give place" to God's wrath when the nations surrounding Israel were harassing the Jews for rebuilding the wall in Jerusalem. Nehemiah prayed what's known as an "imprecatory prayer," calling down God's vengeance on His enemies.

> Hear, O our God, for we are despised; turn their reproach on their own heads, and give them as plunder to a land of captivity! Do not cover their iniquity, and do not let their sin be blotted out from before You; for they have provoked You to anger before the builders . . . My God, remember Tobiah and Sanballat, according to these their works, and the prophetess Noadiah and the rest of the prophets who would have made me afraid (Nehemiah 4:4–5; 6:14).

When Paul was a prisoner in Rome, he prayed to "give place" to God's wrath in his second letter to Timothy, saying, "Alexander the coppersmith did me much harm. May the Lord repay him according to his works" (2 Timothy 4:14).

The best examples come from King David's imprecatory prayers in the Psalms. Look at Psalm 69 to see how David prayed to "give place" to God's wrath. David starts by acknowledging the pain the offenses were causing him.

> Save me, O God!
> For the waters have come up to *my* neck.
> I sink in deep mire,
> Where *there is* no standing;
> I have come into deep waters,
> Where the floods overflow me.
> I am weary with my crying;
> My throat is dry;
> My eyes fail while I wait for my God (Psalm 69:1–3).

Then David names the offenses people were committing against him. Notice he doesn't generalize the offenses; he's specific about each one.

> Those who hate me without a cause
> Are more than the hairs of my head;
> They are mighty who would destroy me,
> *Being* my enemies wrongfully;
> Though I have stolen nothing,
> I *still* must restore *it* . . .

> Those who sit in the gate speak against me,
> And I *am* the song of the drunkards (Psalm 69:4,12).

Next, David talks about his anger. You can almost feel the emotion in what he writes. "Let their table become a snare before them, And their well-being a trap. Let their eyes be darkened, so that they do not see; And make their loins shake continually" (Psalm 69:22–23). Finally, he asks God to take vengeance on those who committed the offenses against him, saying, "Pour out Your indignation upon them, And let Your wrathful anger take hold of them" (Psalm 69:24).

We can see the essential parts of a prayer that "gives place to" or transfers an offense to God's wrath in these prayers. They are:

1. Naming the offense and the person who committed it.
2. Acknowledging the anger, pain, and injury the offense produced.
3. Declaring your transfer of the right of vengeance to God.

Several Christian authors have written transfer prayers. Neil Anderson (1996), in his book *Freedom from Addiction,* R.T. Kendall (2007) in his book *Total Forgiveness,* and Dr. Gary Chapman (1999), in his book *The Other Side of Love: Handling Anger in a Godly Way* all teach the use of a releasing transfer prayer. Dr. Chapman calls his prayer the "Prayer of Release." I've placed the numbered points from the above list into Dr. Chapman's prayer to show where they're used.

> God,
> (1) You know what _____ did when
> _____. (2) You know how much it hurt
> me. (3) You tell me in your word that I shouldn't
> avenge myself, so I'm letting you take care of this. I
> give you the offense, the anger, and the pain of what
> _____ did. You do what needs to be done with
> this person. Thank you for taking the offense, anger,
> and pain of what _____ did. Help me to not let
> this bother me anymore. Amen.[6]

If you pray this prayer from a sincere heart and make a genuine decision to transfer an offense to God, God will free you from the burden of the offense and the pain the offense caused. Likewise, you give God the authority to exercise His wrath on your behalf. You may wonder how God carries out His wrath in the life of the person whose offense you release to Him. How does it work?

I had a chance to see God's wrath firsthand with a man I was counseling. Sam called and told me he'd argued with his father. His father was so angry that he told Sam he never liked him, that Sam was a terrible child, and that he wished Sam had never been born. Sam was crushed. He came over, and we discussed the situation to see what he should do. We agreed that Sam should pray an imprecatory prayer of transfer. Sam prayed Dr. Chapman's Prayer of Release and was relieved of the burden of the experience.

I thought that was the end, but Sam called a few days later with great news. God's wrath worked on his father's heart so much that his father apologized for the things he said and asked for forgiveness. The apology was even more remarkable because Sam had never heard his father apologize to anyone in 50 years. God's vengeance is always consistent with His loving character. Isaiah 54:8 says it best: "'With a little wrath I hid My face from you for a moment; But with everlasting kindness, I will have mercy on you,' Says the Lord, your Redeemer."

Understand me, there are sins we must confront and even sins we can't allow in the church, such as fornication and uncleanness (Ephesians 5:3–4), but the Bible also teaches that some sins should be overlooked.

> The discretion of a man makes him slow to anger, And his glory *is* to overlook a transgression. Proverbs 19:11
>
> Hatred stirs up strife, but love covers all sins. Proverbs 10:12
>
> And above all things have fervent love for one another, for '*love will cover a multitude of sins.*' 1 Peter 4:8

Sometimes people say unkind words while they're sick—like Debbie in the previous chapter—or in the middle of a crisis. In these cases, confronting them would be inappropriate. Do you want someone confronting you every time you sin?

Transferring an offense to God doesn't let people off the hook for what they've done to you; it puts the offense into the hands of Someone who can do something about it. Transferring an offense also doesn't mean you can't confront the person; it only means you don't have to live with the offense's pain while waiting for an apology. Here's a step-by-step look at how transferring an offense works:

- Someone commits an offense against you.
- Your spirit is exasperated or provoked.

- You experience anger and/or pain that alerts you to the offense.
- A barrier is created between you and the person who offended you (Proverbs 18:19).
- You decide the best thing to do in this circumstance is to "give place," to transfer the "position of authority" to God's wrath so that He can deal with the person and the offense on your behalf.
- You pray an imprecatory prayer that includes these elements:
    1. Naming the offense and the person who committed it.
    2. Acknowledging the anger, pain, and injury the offense produced.
    3. Declaring your transfer of the right of vengeance to God.

You don't pray a general prayer like, "God, you know what happened; please take care of it." You are specific and name the offense and the person who committed it. You deal with offenses one at a time, especially if there's a situation where there are several offenses. You pray from your heart, remembering that just reading the prayer won't do anything. Then God heals you of the pain and works in a way consistent with His loving character.

Here's a sample of what our friend Bret would pray. God, (1) You know what *Carl* did when he *called me a freeloader*. (2) You know how much it hurt me. (3) You tell me in Your Word that I shouldn't avenge myself, so I'm letting You take care of this. I give You the offense, the anger, and the pain of what *Carl* did. You do what needs to be done with this person. Thank You for taking the offense, anger, and pain of what *Carl* did. Help me to not let this bother me anymore. Amen.[7] If Bret had prayed this prayer, he may have been able to overlook Carl's offense and stay at Eastside.

The point: You can avoid giving the devil a foothold in your life by transferring offenses to God. You can transfer offenses to

God by praying an imprecatory prayer that names the offense and the person who committed it, acknowledges the anger, pain, and injury the offense produced, and declares your transfer of the right of vengeance to Him. When you pray this prayer from a sincere heart, God frees you from the pain and anger the offense produced and frees you to deal with the person who offended you in a way consistent with His loving character.

## Conclusion

To stop living the way you did before you were saved and start living the life God intends, you must use anger properly. God gives you the tool of transfer to deal with the anger you have from an offense you can't or shouldn't confront or when you don't get a sincere apology. God wants you to put off your old way of sinning in your anger and put on the new way of dealing with it properly by confronting, forgiving, and transferring the offenses you can't resolve to Him. Transfer isn't always the best choice in dealing with conflict, but it's an essential tool if you're going to keep from giving the devil a foothold in your life.


God wants you to change by:


<u>Putting off the old</u>     and     <u>Putting on the new</u>
Abusing Anger                           Using Anger


## Releasing Exercise

Do you have any painful memories?

Take a moment and think of a painful memory that comes to your mind. Put the details of it into the appropriate spaces in the Prayer of Release on the next page. Be specific about what the person did. Try to describe it in practical terms, not theologically. Here are some examples:

Use a practical description of what the person did:

> Mary told Debbie I stole from the church food pantry.

Avoid theological descriptions:

> Mary gossiped about me.

Once you've written the details in the Prayer of Release, pray the Prayer of Release right now.

---

God,

You know what _____ did, when _____

                   (Name)                   (What he/she did)

_____. You know how much it hurt me. You tell me in Your Word that I shouldn't avenge myself, so I'm letting you take care of this. I give You the offense, the anger, and the pain of what _____ did.

                                                  (Name)

You do what needs to be done with this person. Thank You for taking the offense, anger, and pain of what _____ did.

                                                (Name)

Help me to not let this bother me anymore. Amen.[8]

---

## Memorize these verses:

"Be angry and do not sin, do not let the sun go down on your wrath, nor give place to the devil." (Ephesians 4:26)

"So then, my beloved brethren, let every man be swift to hear, slow to speak, slow to wrath; for the wrath of man does not produce the righteousness of God." (James 1:19–20)

"Beloved, do not avenge yourselves, but *rather* give place to wrath; for it is written, '*Vengeance is Mine, I will repay*,' says the Lord." (Romans 12:19)

Discussion Questions

1. Do you have any thoughts or questions about this chapter?

2. How did you know when a conflict was over in your family growing up?

3. What do you usually say when someone apologizes to you?

4. Whom have you confronted, or who has confronted you in the past?

5. When have you gotten or heard an insincere apology from someone?

6. Where can you apply the Prayer of Release in your relationships right now?

# 7

# Put off Stealing

*"Let him who stole steal no longer" (Ephesians 4:28a)*

## 1. To stop stealing, you need to know why it's wrong

*"Let him who stole steal no longer . . ." (Ephesians 4:28a)*

Larry loved his job as the rental department manager at the local hardware store. He enjoyed teaching his friends and neighbors how to use the rental tools to fix toilets, pressure wash their houses, and care for their lawns. While it wasn't the most glamorous job, his customers appreciated his help as much as he enjoyed helping them.

Larry was also a very conscientious worker. Whenever he needed to use a piece of equipment from the rental department, he would ask permission from his boss before taking it. When a big hardware chain bought out the store, he tried to fit in with the new management.

Late one evening, after the store closed and the registers shut down, Larry remembered he needed a roll of duct tape for a project he wanted to finish that night. Larry took a roll of duct tape off the shelf, put it into his lunchbox, and left. The following day Larry showed up for work as usual, but he noticed the other employees were staring at him, not in a good way. Larry started his normal routine when the new store manager opened her office door and called him in. She shut the door and asked Larry to sit down. Larry wasn't sure what was happening, but he knew something was wrong. His manager took out a computer tablet, put it in front of him, and hit play. Larry was shocked to see a video of himself walking up to the duct tape shelf, grabbing a roll, and putting it into his lunch box.

Larry's manager looked him in the eyes and asked, "Did you pay for that, Larry?" Larry's mind raced as he thought, *What have I done?* Finally, with his head down, Larry answered, "No." Larry's manager asked if he'd taken anything else. As Larry thought about his years at the store, he realized that he'd taken a handful of nails or a couple of screws here and there but had never thought anything of it. He never took anything significant, just little things he needed around the house. He tried to explain but was overwhelmed with grief when he left.

The store manager suspended Larry until she could discuss the situation with the regional supervisor. He returned to the manager's office a week later, waiting to hear his fate. The store manager said, "Larry, the regional supervisor decided to put you on six-month probation and demote you to a stocker. You must understand that this store doesn't tolerate stealing, no matter how small. If this happens again, you'll be fired on the spot."

While it may not seem like a big issue, stealing is the next important thing Paul wants you to put off to be ready for Christ to use. Stealing is taking something that belongs to someone else without getting the owner's permission. According to the online encyclopedia Encarta, you can steal by taking or getting something secretly, surreptitiously, through trickery, or by taking credit for something someone else has created, like their ideas, theories, or writings presented as your own.

One of the Bible's best-known references to stealing is in the Ten Commandments, where God says, "Thou shalt not steal" (Exodus 20:15). Unfortunate, there are many accounts of stealing in the Bible. When we looked at the story of Jacob and Esau in Chapter 3, we focused on the lies Jacob told his father, but the story is also about stealing. Jacob stole Esau's blessing.

Beyond the things already listed by Encarta, you can steal God's words and ideas, as the false prophets did in Jeremiah 23:30. You can steal people's hearts away from God's appointed leader, as Absalom stole the hearts of King David's subjects in 2 Samuel 15:6.

You can even steal the affection of other people's spouses, as Solomon warns about in Proverbs 9:17.

The Bible gives several reasons why stealing is wrong. First, stealing is wrong because it violates God's plan to bless people through their work. When God created Adam, He "took the man and put him in the garden of Eden to tend and keep it" (Genesis 2:15). God wanted Adam to work in the garden so he would experience the blessing of receiving the fruit of his labor.

Fortunately, this blessing didn't end when Adam sinned. Solomon says in Ecclesiastes 3:12, "I know that nothing is better for them than to rejoice, and to do good in their lives, and also that every man should eat and drink and enjoy the good of all his labor—it is the gift of God." Paul reaffirms this fact when he says God "richly provides us with everything to enjoy" (1 Timothy 6:17). God gave us the blessing of fruit-producing work to enjoy life here on Earth. Stealing is wrong because when you take what a person works to get, you take away their ability to enjoy the God-given fruits of their labor.

Next, stealing is wrong because it violates God's plan of ownership. When Peter confronted Ananias and Sapphira for lying about the price of the land they sold in Acts 5:4, he said, "While it remained, was it not your own? And after it was sold, was it not in your own control?" Peter clearly says Ananias and Sapphira owned their property and had the right to do what they wanted with it. Stealing is wrong because when you take something from someone without their permission, you violate their God-given right to decide what's done with their possessions.

Finally, stealing is wrong because it violates God's command to be content. God commands you to be content in Hebrews 13:5, saying, "Let your conduct be without covetousness; be content with such things as you have. For He Himself has said, 'I will never leave you nor forsake you.'"

Paul describes what it means to be content when he thanks the Philippian Christians for a gift they sent him. Look at what he says:

> Not that I speak in regard to need, for I have learned in whatever state I am, to be content: I know how to be abased, and I know how to abound. Everywhere and in all things I have learned both to be full and to be hungry, both to abound and to suffer need. I can do all things through Christ who strengthens me (4:11–13).

According to Paul, contentment is basing your happiness on Christ's presence and work in your life, not on what you have. It didn't matter to Paul whether he had a juicy steak or nothing at all for dinner. He was happy he had Christ and trusted that Christ would give him the strength to do the right thing regardless of his menu.

On the other hand, Obadiah directly connects stealing and the feeling of not having enough. Obadiah says in Obadiah 1:5, "If thieves had come to you, If robbers by night . . . Would they not have stolen till they had enough?" According to Obadiah, thieves steal because they think they don't have enough. According to Dictionary.com, this "restless desire or craving for something one does not have" is discontentment. Paul warns about the dangers of discontent in 1 Timothy 6:6–10:

> Now godliness with contentment is great gain. For we brought nothing into this world, and it is certain we can carry nothing out. And having food and clothing, with these we shall be content. But those who desire to be rich fall into temptation and a snare, and into many foolish and harmful lusts which drown men in destruction and perdition. For the love of money is a root of all kinds of evil, for which some

have strayed from the faith in their greediness, and pierced themselves through with many sorrows.

Stealing is wrong because when you take things from others, you're looking for happiness in things instead of in the presence and work of Christ in your life.

You may not think stealing is serious because most things you steal are of little value, like a box of paper clips, but stealing can cause more harm than you realize. Stealing can lead you to commit other sins. In John 12, Judas complained about a jar of perfume a woman used to anoint Jesus' feet. He accused her of wasting the perfume and said she should have sold it for money to feed the poor. However, at the end of the account, we learn that Judas, the one in charge of the moneybag, really wanted to sell the perfume so he could steal from the profits. Stealing helped make Judas one of the worst hypocrites of all time.

If stealing goes unchecked, it can become a part of the culture of your church or organization. When Jesus went to the temple in Mark 11:15, He turned over the money tables and drove out the vendors because they had turned the whole temple organization into a "den of thieves."

Stealing can even lead you to hurt people physically. People who steal tend to depersonalize those they steal from, seeing them as barriers to their happiness. The more a person steals, the more they depersonalize others. People who steal don't realize that the more they depersonalize those around them, the easier it is to hurt them. Eventually, thieves can lose their ability to empathize with the people they're stealing from and remorse for what they do to them. The robbers in Jesus's story about the Good Samaritan did just that when they beat their victim and left him for dead (Luke 10:30).

While working my way through Bible College, I worked in a convenience store. One night while I was working the third shift. At about 3 a.m., a man came in wearing dark sunglasses with his hand in his coat pocket. He pushed the pocket toward me and said, "Give me all the money." I quickly opened the cash register and gave him the money. But instead of leaving with the money, he told me to lie across the counter. As I put my head down on the counter, I was sure he would shoot me. He pulled the gun from his pocket and hit me with it twice instead, once on the head and once on the neck. He probably thought he was doing me a favor by not shooting me, for which I am grateful, but I suffered for years from the emotional and physical injuries he caused. I doubt he started hitting people over the head with a gun as a toddler. It was more likely a change that happened slowly over a lifetime of stealing. If you've been stealing from people and continue to do so, you may become so calloused to the needs of others that, like the thieves in the story of the Good Samaritan or the man who pistol-whipped me, you may maim or kill to get what you want.

Stealing may also cost you personally. You may face social consequences when you're caught stealing like my friend Larry at the beginning of this chapter. You may also face criminal charges. It may even cost you your life. Achan probably thought it was insignificant when he took the treasure that God had claimed for His own from Jericho in Joshua 7:11, but he had to pay with his life.

However, the most severe consequences of stealing are the ones you face when you die. Paul says, "Do you not know that the unrighteous will not inherit the kingdom of God? Do not be deceived. Neither fornicators, nor idolaters, nor adulterers, nor homosexuals, nor sodomites, nor thieves, nor covetous, nor drunkards, nor revilers, nor extortioners will inherit the kingdom of God" (1 Corinthians 6:9–10). Apart from Christ's forgiveness when you receive and believe in Him, stealing one thing is enough to keep you from heaven. Stealing is a serious thing in the eyes of God.

The point: Stealing is taking something that belongs to someone else without permission. Stealing is wrong, whether material possessions, ideas, or relationships. Stealing is wrong because it takes away people's ability to enjoy the blessing of the fruits of their labor and their God-given right to do what they want with their possessions. It also violates God's command to be content with what He has given you. Stealing can do more harm than just depriving people of their possessions. It can lead to more sin against the person you steal from and a more significant loss for you.

## 2. To stop stealing, you need to repent

Once you realize stealing is wrong, you have a choice to make. Paul says there are two ways you can respond to your sin in 2 Corinthians 7:10: "For godly sorrow produces repentance *leading* to salvation, not to be regretted; but the sorrow of the world produces death." The first and best way to respond to your sin is with "godly sorrow" that "produces repentance." Paul describes the Corinthian church's godly sorrow in the next verse.

- "What clearing of yourselves" - They were committed to making amends.
- "What indignation" - They were angry about what they had done and the pain they had caused by their actions.
- "What fear" - They had godly fear of the possible consequences they faced for having broken God's laws.
- "What vehement desire" - They were willing to do whatever it took.
- "What zeal" - They were tireless and relentless in their efforts.
- "What vindication" - They stuck to it until they succeeded in doing everything they could to make up for what they had done. (2 Corinthians 7:11)

"In all *things,*" Paul said, they proved themselves "to be clear in this matter" (2 Corinthians 7:11).

The second and unproductive response to your sin is "the sorrow of the world" that "produces death." Jesus describes this sor-

94

row when He says, "Men loved darkness rather than light, because their deeds were evil. For everyone practicing evil hates the light and does not come to the light, lest his deeds should be exposed" (John 3:19b–20). Worldly sorrow causes you to hide from your sin and its consequences.

The prophet Jeremiah talks about this kind of worldly sorrow when he says, "the thief is ashamed when he is found out" (Jeremiah 2:26). The word shame describes the feelings of humiliation and disgrace at being caught, not sorrow for what was done [1] Shame keeps you from taking responsibility for your actions. If you're only ashamed when you're caught stealing, you'll probably steal again. However, God can transform you and give you victory over stealing if you have godly sorrow. That's what happened to the tax collector Zacchaeus when he met Jesus. Zacchaeus stood up and said, "Look, Lord, I give half of my goods to the poor; and if I have taken anything from anyone by false accusation, I restore fourfold" (Luke 19:8). Jesus answered and said, "Today salvation has come to this house" (Luke 19:9). If you've been stealing from others, you need to repent and show godly sorrow just like Zacchaeus by:

- Being committed to making it right.
- Feeling anger about what you've done and the pain you've caused by your actions.
- Feeling godly fear for the possible consequences you face for having broken God's laws.
- Being willing to do whatever it takes.
- Being tireless and relentless in your efforts.
- Sticking to it until you succeed in doing everything possible to make up for what you've done.

The Point: To stop stealing you need to have the godly sorrow Paul talks about in 2 Corinthians 7. Godly sorrow brings a desire to deal with the consequences of your sin. Godly sorrow brings repentance and life, while worldly sorrow brings death.

## Conclusion

To be prepared for Jesus to use in the church, you must stop stealing. You need to understand what the Bible says about stealing, that it's wrong and hurts both you and the people from whom you steal. The first step in overcoming stealing is repenting with godly sorrow.

God wants you to change by:

<u>Putting off the old</u>      and      <u>Putting on the new</u>
Stealing

Discussion Questions

1. Do you have any thoughts or questions about this chapter?

2. When have you stolen something?

3. What were the consequences?

4. When have you had something stolen from you?

5. How did that make you feel?

6. Whom have you stolen from that you need to show repentance and godly sorrow toward?

# 8

# Put on Good Work and Generosity

*"... but rather let him labor, working with his hands what is good, that he may have something to give him who has need." (Ephesians 4:28)*

## 1. You need to replace stealing with labor
*Ephesians 4:28 but rather let him labor*

One of Sam's favorite things about church was attending his High School Sunday school class. His teacher Mr. Johnson made the New Testament come alive with the stories of the early church. He never got tired of talking about the Bible with Mr. Johnson.

Sam finally found the courage to ask his parents if he could go to Bible College to become a church history professor. Unfortunately, they didn't have the money to send him to a private school, so he would have to attend a local community college. That following Sunday, Sam wasn't his excited self. After class, Mr. Johnson asked him what was wrong. Sam told him about his conversation with his parents and his disappointment. Mr. Johnson told Sam not to lose hope.

Sam was surprised when Mr. Johnson arrived for dinner a few weeks later. During dinner, Sam's parents explained that Mr. Johnson had met with them to discuss Sam's future. He'd inherited a large sum of money and was looking for some way to invest it in building God's kingdom. Mr. Johnsons smiled and said, "There's no better investment I can think of than to invest in people. I want to pay for your education so you can become a Bible College professor."

Sam's four years at Bible College were filled with successes and challenges. Part of the agreement with Mr. Johnsons was keeping a B average. He worked hard in the classes he liked but did the minimum required in the rest. Fortunately, his A's and C's balanced out.

Mr. Johnson died unexpectedly during the second semester of Sam's senior year. Sam traveled home for the funeral and was deeply saddened by Mr. Johnson's death. Sam finished his senior year and continued living in the city where he attended school. He found a job as a part-time janitor in a local church to make up for the loss of Mr. Johnson's support and secretly slept in the janitor's room to save on rent. He knew he would lose his job if caught, but decided it was worth the risk.

Sam was now faced with funding the rest of his education. He wanted to attend seminary in Europe because they offered the best programs in church history. But how could he pay for it? Sam thought long and hard about his options. He'd never had a job in school and had no marketable skills. He didn't want to put off going to seminary, so he wasn't willing to take the time to learn a skill that would pay enough to support him.

Then Sam saw a post on social media for bartender training. In just three weeks at bartender school, he could learn a skill that would pay enough to support him through seminary. The work seemed easy, so he signed up for the class. Sam was relieved to have such a simple solution to his problem.

Sam desired to serve the Lord, and although he had some struggles, he was making an honest attempt to live out his faith. However, Sam may not have considered that God cares about our work. It isn't enough to want to stop stealing. Paul tells you that to be ready for Christ to use, you must replace stealing with laboring with good work. Doug Sherman and William Hendricks, in their book *Your Work Matters to God,* put it this way,

> Christ is not content to make us good people or even better people; He means to make us new people, people who are like Him. In regard to our work this means that He sets about changing our character, our

motives, our attitude, and our values. The Change is a change of our character. So a thief ...would change from a person who steals to a person who works at honest labor.[1]

According to Paul in Ephesians 4:28, once you put off stealing, you must replace it with "labor." Labor means to wear yourself out "through physical or mental effort."[2] According to Sherman and Hendricks, learning to labor God's way must include developing a godly "workstyle." A godly "workstyle is the way you do your work." It's "the attitudes you express, the methods you employ, and the strategies you use to achieve your results."[3]

The Bible gives several qualities you need to have to labor well with a godly workstyle. A godly workstyle seeks and pursues peace with coworkers. Peter says in 1 Peter 3:10-11 anyone who would "love life and see good days" needs to "turn away from evil and do good... seek peace and pursue it." To seek and pursue peace in labor, you must be in harmony with the people around you and avoid the politics, internal wars, and dissensions that often plague the workplace.[4]

Next, a godly workstyle is thankful. Paul says in Colossians 3:15 that along with letting "God's peace rule in your heart," you need to "be thankful." In his book Business for the Glory of God, Dr. Wayne Grudem gives several reasons why you should be thankful in your work. You can be thankful in your work because it allows you to produce "goods and services for others." You can be thankful in your work because it provides resources you can use "for your own enjoyment." And ultimately, you can be thankful because your work reveals God's goodness as He provides you with a job and the ability to do it.[5]

A godly workstyle also includes an attitude of sincerity. Paul says in Colossians 3:22 that you should avoid the worldly workstyle of "eyeservice" and "men-pleasers." Eyeservice is only working when you're being watched, and man-pleasing is brown-nosing to get on your boss' good side. Paul says you should practice "sincerity of heart, fearing God" instead by being faithful and helpful to your boss even when they aren't looking, and having a pure heart that cares more about pleasing God than men.[6]

Paul says in Ephesians 6:7 that a godly workstyle involves being good-willed toward your employer and coworkers. You can be good-willed to your employer and coworkers by having a favorable or sympathetic attitude, being friendly, staying connected with them, and meeting them halfway.[7]

A godly workstyle works "heartily, as to the Lord and not to men." The word "heartily" literally means "from the soul" (Colossians 3:23-24). Working heartily "from the soul" can be hard when your boss is lazy or a tyrant. So instead of thinking that you're working for your boss or supervisor, you should work as though you are working for Jesus. When you're working heartily for Jesus, you can be obedient (Ephesians 6:5) and submissive regardless of how you're treated (1 Peter 2:18). Working for Jesus allows you to abide by the rules and policies of your company and carry out the orders of those above you despite your circumstances.[8]

A godly workstyle applies to bosses as well. When Paul describes a boss' godly workstyle, he says, "And you, masters, do the same things to them" (Ephesians 6:9). As a boss, you need to seek peace and pursue it, be thankful, and have goodwill toward your employees by having a favorable or sympathetic disposition, being friendly, staying connected, and meeting them half-way (Ephesians 6:9).[9] You must also work heartily as to the Lord (Colossians 3:23-24) and be as sincere (Colossians 3:22) as your employees.

On top of that, a boss' godly workstyle needs to be just and fair (Colossians 4:1) without threatening (Ephesians 6:9), remembering that as a "master," you also have a master in heaven (Ephesians 6:9). According to Grudem,

> If others work for us, we need to think of them as
> equal in value as human beings made in the image of

God, and our heart's desire should be that the job bring them good and not harm. We should be thankful to God for the money and profit, but we should never love money or profit. We are to love God and our neighbor instead.[10]

The Point: To put off stealing, you need to put on laboring. Laboring combines working hard with a godly workstyle. God defines a godly workstyle for both employees and employers. An employee's godly workstyle seeks and pursues peace, is thankful, sincere, good-willed, and works heartily as to the Lord and not to men. An employer's godly workstyle includes the same qualities as an employee's, plus being just and fair, not threatening, and remembering that as a "master," you also have a master in heaven.

## 2. To labor well, you need to do good work
*working with his hands what is good,*

Depending on your work experiences, you may see work as bad. But regardless of your experiences, God's plan for work is good. How do I know this? When God created Adam, Genesis 2:15 says He "put him in the garden of Eden to tend and keep it." "Tend" means to *work* by *tilling the ground.*[11] Since this was before Adam sinned, the summary God made when He "saw everything that He had made, and indeed *it was* very good" applies to Adam's work (Genesis 1:31). Work only became toil as a part of the consequences of Adam's sin (Genesis 3:17-18). Even though work is harder than it was before Adam sinned, you were created with a God-given "desire to do well and to improve what [you] are able to do."[12]

Good work is consistent with God's commands, makes "a positive contribution to society," and "serves others by doing good for them."[13] But as you saw in the story of Sam becoming a bartender to pay for his seminary education, figuring out whether work is good or not can be challenging. According to Sherman, legitimate or good work is also work God uses "to meet the needs of people."[14] The Bible mentions many kinds of work people did to meet the needs of others: baker (Genesis 40:5), butler (Genesis 40:21), cook (1 Samuel 9:23-24), grinder or miller (Matthew 24:41), fisherman (Isaiah 19:8), hunter (Jeremiah 16:16), shepherd (Luke 2:8), herdsman (Genesis 4:20), farmer (Genesis 4:2), and harvestman (Isaiah 17:5) to name a few.[15] Good work can take on many forms in today's world as well. Consider the food you eat. Sherman describes the many people and jobs it takes just to put breakfast on your table.

> God has used a rather extensive system of workers to give us this food. He has used farmers to plant and cultivate citrus trees and wheat, and to raise dairy cows. We might also mention the scientists who have checked the food for purity and the bankers who have arranged for the financing. Then, too, there are the dealers of farm equipment, and behind them the builders of that equipment. Then we should remember the trucks and their drivers that God used to haul this food our way. And we should appreciate the truck stop operators along the way who have provided diesel fuel and coffee. And, of course, someone had to lay down those miles of interstate that connect our country. And we should thank God for the supermarket employee, for the guy who carries the bag to our car, and for the wife [or husband] that puts it all on the table.[16]

Each of these jobs and those who do them are significant because meeting people's needs is significant and contributes "directly to God's work in the world." Sometimes the connection to meeting people's needs isn't so obvious. What about someone who builds pallets, writes computer code, is a comedian, or is a stockbroker? While job's like these may appear disconnected from anything that serves people, they often do. "To find the contribution requires us to think broadly about the web of relationships God uses to meet human needs."[17]

One important factor in doing good work is finding a job for which you're suited. Your talents, abilities, experiences, personality, and temperament all play a part in making up who you are as a worker. An article titled *A Better Way to Train Up A Child* from Pastor Chuck Swindoll's Insight for Living Ministries describes how Proverbs 22:6 reveals our uniqueness when it says, "Train up a child in the way he should go, And when he is old he will not depart from it." When Proverbs 22:6 challenges parents to help train their children "in the way they should go," it's referring to what can be described as their "characteristic manner."[18] Some children are artistic, "others athletic, and still others academic. One may be strong-willed. Another compliant. One child can be encouraged by rewards or recognition. At the same time, another couldn't care less."[19] For a parent to train up their child well, they need to understand their child's "characteristic manner" and move them in that direction. The same can be said for decisions about your career choices. God gave you greater strengths and talents in one area and other people greater strengths and talents in another.[20] Seeking a job that uses your strengths and talents is one way to find "the way you should go."

What if you don't know your talents, abilities, and gifts? Fortunately, the modern work industry is based on a competitive system that tests your abilities. When you find something you do better than others, you're paid for it.[21] When someone else can do something better than you, you're not. Dr. Grudem tells about a careless painter he hired once for his house. "He lasted only a day…The world is so diverse, and the economic system has so many needs, that I am sure there is some area in which he can fulfill a need and do it well. But it wasn't painting."[22] When you can't do a particular job, you may see yourself as a failure and want to give up. Or you can be like Thomas Edison, who said, "I have not failed 10,000 times—I've successfully

found 10,000 ways that will not work."[23] When you can't do a particular job, move into another field.

If you need help discovering what your "characteristic manner" is, several websites offer tests to help identify it. Here are a few
to help you get started.

www.yourfreecareertest.com/
www.mynextmove.org/explore/ip
www.opencolleges.edu.au/careers/career-quiz

What do you do when jobs are scarce and you can't find a job
consistent with your "characteristic manner?" Sometimes doing a job
you don't enjoy is the "way you should go." Through the years, I
worked several jobs I didn't enjoy because I had to pay the bills.
When you can't find a job that's consistent with your "characteristic
manner," look for one that's consistent with God's commands and
where you can "make a positive contribution to society" and "that
serves others by doing good for them."[24] Even the most unpleasant
job can give glory to God when you use a godly workstyle.

Whether your job is a dream or a nightmare, the good works
you do there are a part of God's purpose for your life. Ephesians
2:10 says that God designed you for good works that he planned for
you to do long before you were born. The good works he plans aren't
just the big things. "Good works includes anything we do in life that
honors God, that fits the way he created us and intends for us to
live."[25] Even something as simple as serving people can be a part of
the good works God wants you to do, whether it's your boss, your
coworkers, or the people you serve while doing your job. "No matter
how boring and insignificant your work seems, God doesn't view
your work as insignificant… He regards your job and you with great
dignity and value. So should you!"[26] "The idea that God is using you
to accomplish a specific purpose can be a real help if you question
the significance of your career."[27]

The Point: Laboring also includes doing good work. Good work is consistent with God's commands and work He uses "to meet the needs of people." It's important to try and find work suited to your strengths and talents, but there are times when any work consistent with God's word that pays the bills is enough. Even the most menial job can have value when you do it with a godly workstyle for the glory of God.

## 3. To labor well, you need to understand the dangers of earning money

When you replace stealing with laboring and start earning your own money, it can lead to a whole new set of problems. The money you earn from good labor can be used to tempt you to sin.[28] One temptation you may face when you start making money is greediness. Greediness is the longing to satisfy yourself with pleasure and things instead of God (Ephesians 4:19).[29] When you don't have much money, your choices and opportunities for pleasure and material things are few. But when you have more money, your choices and options grow. Unfortunately, many of those choices and opportunities are for "foolish and harmful" pleasures and things that "drown men in destruction and perdition (1 Timothy 6:9)." That's why Paul says the "love of money is a root of all *kinds of* evil" that leads people away from their faith and pierces them "through with many sorrows (1 Timothy 6:10)."

Another temptation is to be proud, thinking that you, not God, are responsible for what you have.[30] Paul told Timothy to "Command those who are rich in this present age not to be haughty, nor to trust in uncertain riches but in the living God, who gives us richly all things to enjoy (1 Timothy 6:17)." Pride can lead to unhealthy competitiveness that causes you to work excessively, leaving you with no time for rest, or time with family or God. Competitiveness can also keep you from enjoying the fruits of your labor.[31]

You may be tempted to become a hoarder, laying up for yourself treasures on earth and then constantly working to protect your hoard from decay and thieves (Matthew 6:19-21). You may even fall into stealing again by not paying the people who work for you a living wage (James 5:1-6). On the other hand, if you're income doesn't increase enough, you may be tempted to covet what your neighbor has and become an idolater (Exodus 20:17, Colossians 3:5). Jesus described the problem perfectly when he said, "No one can serve two masters; for either he will hate the one and love the other, or else he will be loyal to the one and despise the other. You cannot serve God and mammon." (Matthew 6:24).

The Point: Replacing stealing with laboring and doing good work is an essential step in getting ready for Christ to use, but the money you earn can lead you into greediness, pride, unhealthy competitiveness, hoarding, stealing from the people who work for you by not paying a living wage, and covetousness.

## 4. To avoid the danger of earning money, you need to be generous

*Ephesians 4:28 that he may have something to give him who has need.*

Paul adds another condition for getting victory over stealing. You must become a generous giver who gives to people in need. Paul includes giving to people in need because generosity will protect you from greediness and holding too tightly to the things and pleasures your money can buy. It also keeps you from pride by helping you see the poor with eyes of compassion and not contempt. Finally, it protects you from coveting by keeping your eyes on those who have less instead of those who have more. According to Dr. Grudem, "Those who are rich have more opportunities and also more obligation to give generously to the poor and to the work of the church."[32] That's why Paul tells Timothy to tell the rich to do good and be rich in good works, being ready to give to the poor and share with those in need. (1 Timothy 6:18). "The overwhelming thrust of the Scriptures is that as God sees fit to prosper us, our abundance should begin to spill over and start benefiting others who, for a variety of reasons, are in need."[33]

God values giving to the needy so much that when He described what a godly person looks like, in Ezekiel 18:7–9, He identified giving as a central character trait.

> "If he has not oppressed anyone,
>> But has restored to the debtor his pledge;
> Has robbed no one by violence,
>> But has given his bread to the hungry
>> And covered the naked with clothing;
> If he has not exacted usury nor taken any increase,
>> But has withdrawn his hand from iniquity
>> And executed true judgment between man and man;
> If he has walked in My statutes And kept My judgments faithfully—
> He is just;
> He shall surely live!"
> Says the Lord God.

One challenge in helping people in need is doing it without harming anyone. Remember, Paul's command is to "give to him who has need" (Ephesians 4:28). The needy person isn't someone who doesn't have everything they want. The needy person has actual want of what they need to survive. Jesus told His disciples to practice this kind of generosity in Luke 3:11 when "He answered and said to them, 'He who has two tunics, let him give to him who has none; and he who has food, let him do likewise.'" But Paul also told the Thessalonians that when people won't work, the church shouldn't give them food to eat, calling them disorderly (2 Thessalonians 3:10).

When I was in Bible College, my only source of income was a part-time job helping care for an elderly man. The job wasn't too demanding, so along with going to school, I could also serve as a volunteer intern pastor in the junior high ministry at my church. I bought a motorcycle from the junior high youth pastor's parents with a down payment and an agreement to make regular payments. Unfortunately, I lost my job before I could pay off the motorcycle. I went to the youth pastor and asked what I should do, secretly hoping that he would cancel the debt. After thinking it over, he said, "I could pay off the motorcycle for you, but it would be better for you to quit being an intern, get a job, and pay it off yourself." I was devastated! Not only had I lost my job, but I also lost my intern position. It took me months to recover from that experience, but in the long run, he was right. I developed a sense of personal financial responsibility that's guided me ever since. Who knows if I would have ever learned that lesson and the importance of distinguishing between those who need and those who want if that pastor had given me the money? So before you give money to people, take the time to find out if they're really in need.

When you work hard to make money, you can appreciate what you have and make a difference by giving some of the money you worked hard to earn to help the genuinely needy person. Giving to the needy person helps move you away from your old, depersonalized view of people and allows you to empathize with fellow human beings. This is the life God wants you to live.

Sherman sums up this section well with what he calls a balanced lifestyle of work:

1. God gives you work as the means to provide for yourself [34]

Genesis 1:29 And God said, "See, I have given you every herb *that* yields seed which *is* on the face of all the earth, and every tree whose fruit yields seed; to you it shall be for food.

2. God wants every worker to benefit from the fruit of their labor [35]

Ecclesiastes 5:18-19 Here is what I have seen: *It is* good and fitting *for one* to eat and drink, and to enjoy the good of all his labor in which he toils under the sun all the days of his life which God gives him; for it *is* his heritage.[19] As for every man to whom God has given riches and wealth, and given him power to eat of it, to receive his heritage and rejoice in his labor--this *is* the gift of God.

3. You need to develop an attitude of contentment, not covetousness [36]

Hebrews 13:5 *Let your* conduct *be* without covetousness; *be* content with such things as you have. For He Himself has said, *"I will never leave you nor forsake you."*

4. You need to pursue a lifestyle of limits, not luxury [37]

Matthew 16:24-26 Then Jesus said to His disciples, "If anyone desires to come after Me, let him deny himself, and take up his cross, and follow Me.[25] For whoever desires to save his life will lose it, but whoever loses his life for My sake will find it.[26] For what profit is it to a man if he gains the whole world, and loses his own soul? Or what will a man give in exchange for his soul?

5. You need to cultivate habits of generosity, not greed [38]

1 John 3:17-18 But whoever has this world's goods, and sees his brother in need, and shuts up his heart from him, how does the love of God abide in him? [18] My little children, let us not love in word or in tongue, but in deed and in truth.

The point: The other side of the right to possessions is the obligation to help needy people. Generosity towards needy people includes the responsibility to determine who needy people are, so you can help those who need it and don't hurt those who don't by enabling their disorderly behavior. Generosity enables you to keep your view of your possessions in its proper perspective and curbs your desire to have more than you should.

## Conclusion

God wants you to stop stealing and start laboring with good work instead. He also wants you to practice giving to people in need for their sake and yours.

You need to stop living like you did before you were saved. For you to change, you need to


God wants you to change by:

<table>
<tr><td>Put off the old</td><td>and</td><td>Put on the new</td></tr>
<tr><td>Stealing</td><td></td><td>Good work and Generosity</td></tr>
</table>


Discussion Questions:

1. Do you have any thoughts or questions about this chapter?



2. When have you helped a needy person or been helped when you were needy?

3. What were your best and worst jobs?

4. Where are your strengths and talents?

5. Who taught you how to work?

6. Who around you is truly needy and could benefit from your generosity?

# 9

# Put off Corrupt Words

*"Let no corrupt word proceed out of your mouth." (Ephesians 4:29)*


## 1. You need to stop using corrupt words because they are an offense to God

*"Let no corrupt word proceed out of your mouth." (Ephesians 4:29)*

During my career as a pastor, I sometimes worked other jobs to supplement my pastoral income. One of those jobs was working as a carpenter. Carpentry gave me opportunities to work with all kinds of interesting people. There were architects, engineers, interior and exterior designers, landscapers, electricians, audio–video technicians, painters, drywallers, plumbers, and so on. Each person was as different as the job they did. One of my favorite people was an electrician who loved to whistle. The only problem was that he was tone-deaf. He happily whistled the same tuneless song all day long for days on end.

Some noises, however, weren't as easy to put up with. We had worked on a new house for several weeks when the plumbers arrived. Usually, this was a good thing, but the boss of the plumbing crew started complaining about the conditions on the job site as soon as he walked in the door. Worse than the complaining, though, was the swearing. He swore about having to work alongside the electricians and the heating and cooling crews. He swore about the weather. He even swore about the shoddy job his workers were doing.

After a week or so, he found out I was a pastor. He sat beside me at lunch and told me he went to a church in a nearby town. I told him I knew of the church. Then he told me he'd been a deacon in the church for years. I don't know if he saw the shock on my face, but

I'm sure it was nothing compared to the look of disgust I saw on the face of one of his workers. Miraculously, his language changed on the spot and stayed pretty clean for the rest of the job.

Your language, accent, and even the words you use are shaped by the people you grew up with. What the plumber didn't know, and you may not either, is that your words and how you use them matter to God. One reason your words matter to God is found in an encounter Jesus had with the Pharisees. The Pharisees claimed to be followers of God. They wore Bible verses on their foreheads and hands and even nailed them to their doorposts. Then one day, they accused Jesus of using the power of Satan to do miracles. Jesus warned them about the danger of their words.

> Anyone who speaks a word against the Son of Man, it will be forgiven him; but whoever speaks against the Holy Spirit, it will not be forgiven him, either in this age or in the age to come. Either make the tree good and its fruit good, or else make the tree bad and its fruit bad; for a tree is known by *its* fruit. Brood of vipers! How can you, being evil, speak good things? For out of the abundance of the heart the mouth speaks. A good man out of the good treasure of his heart brings forth good things, and an evil man out of the evil treasure brings forth evil things (Matthew 12:32–35).

The Pharisees made themselves out to be God's servants, but when they used their words to discredit Jesus, they showed themselves as the brood of vipers they were. They claimed to be good "trees," but their words were bad "fruit." God cares about your words because when you claim to be His follower and use corrupt words, you confuse the people around you and bring shame to His name.

Jesus gave another reason your words matter to God when He went on to tell the Pharisees:

> But I say to you that for every idle word men may speak, they will give account of it in the day of judgment. For by your words you will be justified, and by your words you will be condemned. (Matthew 12:36–37)

God hears every word you say, whether you shout them from the rooftop or mumble them under your breath, and He records and holds you accountable for every single one.

The point: You need to be careful about what you say because when you claim to be a Christian but use corrupt words, you give God a bad name, and God holds you accountable for every idle word.

## 2. You need to stop using corrupt words because they hurt the people around you

The next thing God wants you to put off to be ready for Christ to use is corrupt words. You may not realize it, but many of the words you learned to use and the things you learned to say before you were saved are corrupt, bringing death instead of life to the people who hear them.

The word "Corrupt" describes something bad, rotten, or putrid, like rotting fruit or spoiled fish.[1] If I were to ask you what *corrupt* words are, you would probably name things like swearing and dirty or racist jokes, and you'd be right. Paul says in Ephesians 5:3–7 that you should never use dirty words or hurtful humor because they're the words used by "the sons of disobedience," and you should "not be partakers with them."

Some corrupt words, however, aren't as obvious. That's why James says talking is so dangerous. When James says anyone who doesn't "stumble" in words is "a perfect man," he isn't telling you how to be perfect (James 3:2). He's saying you can't be perfect in your words because "The tongue is a fire, a world of iniquity," and "it defiles the whole body, and sets on fire the course of nature; and it is set on fire by hell" (James 3:6). What are some subtle ways you're using corrupt words you may not be aware of?

You may be using words that take God's name in vain. When God gave Moses the Ten Commandments, He said, "You shall not take the name of the LORD your God in vain, for the LORD will not hold *him* guiltless who takes His name in vain (Exodus 20:7). When you use phrases like "Oh, my God" when you're surprised, "Good Lord" when you're upset, or "Jesus Christ" when you're angry, you're words are an offense to God. When you use the names of God or Jesus as an exclamation or an expletive, you're using corrupt words.

You may be using two-faced words. After a run-in with the Pharisees about his disciples not following the custom of washing their hands before they ate, Jesus warned His disciples about two-faced words: "For there is nothing covered that will not be revealed, nor hidden that will not be known. Therefore whatever you have spoken in the dark will be heard in the light, and what you have spoken in the ear in inner rooms will be proclaimed on the housetops" (Luke 12:2–3). This kind of two-faced talking hurts the people around you and dishonors the name of God. When you say one thing to one person and then say the opposite thing to someone else, you're using corrupt words.

You may be using hypocritical words. When Jesus preached to the sermon on the mount, He warned the people about the hypocrisy of self-righteousness, saying, "Hypocrite! First remove the plank from your own eye, and then you will see clearly to remove the speck that is in your brother's eye" (Luke 6:42). It's easier to see sin in other people than it is in yourself. When you make it your job to point out other people's sins without taking care of your own first, you're using hypocritical words to hurt the people God calls you to love.

Maybe you're using flattering words. When Paul wrote to encourage the Thessalonian Christians, he reminded them of how he preached to them: "For neither at any time did we use flattering words, as you know, nor a cloak for covetousness—God *is* witness" (1 Thessalonians 2:5). Paul knew flattery wasn't an appropriate tool when sharing the Gospel because flattery is just another form of worldly manipulation. Flattering people to get something from them or to get on their good side is using corrupt words.

Maybe you're using argumentative words. When Paul wrote to his young student Timothy, he warned about the argumentative person because "he is proud, knowing nothing, but is obsessed with disputes and arguments over words, from which come envy, strife, reviling, evil suspicions" (1 Timothy 6:4). You can become argumentative when you put the need to be right above the need to be loving, or when you're angry with someone and want to punish that person for what they've done. Being quick to argue with people is using corrupt words.

You may be using proud words. When you say things in front of others to make yourself look good or feel better about yourself, you're using corrupt words that hurt others by taking their attention away from God and diverting it to yourself. Paul warned the Christians in Corinth about people who were puffing themselves up, saying, "Now some are puffed up, as though I were not coming to you. But I will come to you shortly, if the Lord wills, and I will know, not the word of those who are puffed up, but the power. For the kingdom of God *is* not in word but in power" (1 Corinthians 4:18–20). If you say things to puff yourself up and get worth, you're using corrupt words.

Maybe you're using demeaning words. The flip side of saying things to puff yourself up is saying something to put others down. The Apostle John was the victim of these kind of corrupt words when Diotrephes put him down in the church. John said,

I wrote to the church, but Diotrephes, who loves to have the preeminence among them, does not receive us. Therefore, if I come, I will call to mind his deeds which he does, prating against us with malicious words. And not content with that, he himself does not receive the brethren, and forbids those who wish to, putting *them* out of the church. 3 John 9–10

The first tool for getting worth is to say or do something to puff yourself up, but if that doesn't work, you may resort to putting others down. You're using corrupt words when you say demeaning things that devalue people, their efforts, and their ideas.

You may be using empty words. When John talked about what it means to be a Christian in the book of 1 John, he questioned the sincerity of the person who claims to be a Christian but isn't backing up their caring words with deeds. He said, "But whoever has this world's goods, and sees his brother in need, and shuts up his heart from him, how does the love of God abide in him? My little children, let us not love in word or in tongue, but in deed and in truth" (1 John 3:17–18). When you don't match your caring words with caring deeds, your empty words hurt the people who need you. Words you say to sound caring without backing them up with loving deeds are corrupt words.

Maybe you're using legalistic words. James warned the Gentile believers about legalism when he wrote a letter to them, saying he "heard that some who went out from us have troubled you with words, unsettling your souls, saying, '*You must* be circumcised and keep the law'—to whom we gave no *such* commandment" (Acts 15:24–29). When you raise your standards of behavior to the standard of godliness, you hurt the people around you. You're using corrupt words when you tell others they need to live up to your standards—standards that don't come from the Bible.

Maybe you're using words of worldly wisdom. Paul refused to use human wisdom when he preached to the Corinthians, saying, "I was with you in weakness, in fear, and in much trembling. And my speech and my preaching *were* not with persuasive words of human wisdom, but in demonstration of the Spirit and of power, that your faith should not be in the wisdom of men but in the power of God" (1 Corinthians 2:3–5). You only weaken your position when you use the world's wisdom to strengthen your arguments. The world's wisdom comes from the same darkened understanding God tells you to stop using in Ephesians 4:17–24, and it hurts the people around you. Your words become corrupt when you elevate human wisdom over God's word.

Maybe you're using words that misinterpret Scripture. Paul warned Timothy about people who mishandle God's Word, saying, "Avoid foolish and ignorant disputes, knowing that they generate strife" (2 Timothy 2:23). When you twist God's words to say what you want, not only are you hurting the people around you, you also risk becoming the focus of God's wrath (2 Peter 1:20; Revelation 22:19). You're using corrupt words when you mishandle God's Word and create strife in the body.

The point: Despite the world's attempts to remove words' meaning, there are corrupt words God doesn't want you to say. Corrupt words are filthy, foolish, or hurtful. They can even be words you hide in humor. You use corrupt words when you take the Lord's name in vain, say one thing publicly and another thing privately, or justify yourself and judge others. Corrupt words are flattering words, argumentative words, words that puff up the person saying them, and words that put others down. They're also words you say that aren't backed by love, promote legalism, elevate human wisdom, or mishandle God's Word and create strife.

## Conclusion

If you continue to use corrupt words you used before you were saved, you will continue to be alienated from the life God wants you to live. You need to stop using corrupt words.

God wants you to change by:

Putting off the old     and     Putting on the new
Corrupt Words

Discussion Questions

1. Do you have any thoughts or questions about this chapter?

2. Where did you learn some of the corrupt words you use?

3. When have corrupt words hurt you? (Please refrain from using names)

4. What corrupt words have you used lately?

5. How do you think the people around you would react if you stopped using corrupt words?

6. Who could you apologize to for using corrupt words?

# 10

# Put on Good Words

*Let no corrupt word proceed out of your mouth, but what is good for necessary edification, that it may impart grace to the hearers. And do not grieve the Holy Spirit of God, by whom you were sealed for the day of redemption. (Ephesians 4:29)*

## 1. God uses your good words to build people up
*". . . but what is good for necessary edification . . ." (Ephesians 4:29)*

There have been many exciting moments in my thirty years as a pastor, from the joys of leading a child to Christ to baptizing a seventy-five-year-old woman who was dedicating her life to serving the Lord. I've also had opportunities to help people navigate through difficult times in their lives, and I've seen God come through for people in ways I could have never imagined. Getting paid to read and study the Bible is also a nice perk.

The life of a pastor isn't always fun and games, however. Whether it's finding the right words to say to a young husband whose wife has died or comforting someone whose child has been tragically taken away by drugs, being a pastor can be heart-wrenching. Some of the most challenging times, however, were when I suffered personal attacks by people I trusted and worked with within the church. One time in particular left me ready to give up being a pastor.

I woke up that Sunday morning, typed my resignation, and put it in my pocket. As I preached what I thought was my last sermon, God started speaking to my heart. The passage I was preaching was about sticking it out through the darkest times in your life. When I was done, I knew I couldn't walk away from the job God had called me to do, so I left my resignation in my pocket and went home. A short time later, a pastor friend called to check on me. I'd left a message telling him I was planning to resign. He was glad I hadn't and said he had a friend who could preach the following Sunday. His friend's name was Dr. Elwood Chipchase, a nationally known speaker and former Bible college president who "just happened" to be in the area and available.

Dr. Chipchase preached a great sermon and then took me out to lunch. He said, "Tracy, you're God's man, and although you may not stay at this church, God has called you to be a pastor." It was amazing to feel the strength of his words and see the confidence he had in me. I realized I was seeking approval as a pastor from people when I really should have been seeking God's. I didn't resign and decided to stick it out through the troubling times. The situation was eventually resolved, and my joy returned. However, none of this would've happened without Dr. Chipchase's encouraging words.

Once you put off your corrupt words and allow God to renew your mind, to be ready for Christ to use you need to replace your corrupt words with good words. There are two things to explore when it comes to good words. Let's start by looking at what "good" is. When the rich young ruler called Jesus "good teacher," in Matthew 19:17, Jesus said, "Why do you call Me good? No one *is* good but One, *that is,* God." According to Jesus, God the Father is the source of goodness. Jesus described God the Father's goodness in the Sermon on the Mount.

> Ask, and it will be given to you; seek, and you will find; knock, and it will be opened to you. For everyone who asks receives, and he who seeks finds, and to him who knocks it will be opened. Or what man is there among you who, if his son asks for bread, will give him a stone? Or if he asks for a fish, will he give him a serpent? If you then, being evil, know how to give good gifts to your children, how much more will

your Father who is in heaven give good things to
those who ask Him! (Matthew 7:7–11)

The good things God the Father gives you are better than the best
things you give to the people you love. God's good is always useful,
beneficial, and profitable. It will never hurt you, although you may
not like it at the time.[1]

The second part of good words is the words themselves. The
Bible records the first words spoken in Genesis 1:3 when God said,
"Let there be light." God is the source of words. Your ability to talk
and communicate with others comes directly from God. Beyond
that, however, is the remarkable fact that God can give you the words
He wants you to say. When Jesus warned His disciples about the
trouble they'd face for being His followers, He promised them that
"the Holy Spirit will teach you in that very hour what you ought to
say" (Luke 12:11).

In the same way, God uses the Holy Spirit to give you good
words to say (Acts 4:31 and 1 Corinthians 2:1–16). The good words
God gives you through the Holy Spirit are always useful, beneficial,
and profitable, and they don't hurt others, although they may not be
welcome at the time.[2] Then, Paul says, God establishes and strengthens your good words to do the work He intended.

Now may our Lord Jesus Christ Himself, and our
God and Father, who has loved us and given *us* everlasting consolation and good hope by grace, comfort
your hearts and establish you in every good word and
work (2 Thessalonians 2:16–17; see also Hebrews
13:20–21).

One way God uses your good words is to edify the church.
The word "edify" literally means "building up a house" and describes
how God builds up the people in the church.[3] Paul gives us a glimpse
of how the Corinthian Christians used their words to build up the

church when he told them, "Whenever you come together, each of you has a psalm, has a teaching, has a tongue, has a revelation, has an interpretation. Let all things be done for edification" (1 Corinthians 14:26).

Edification is other-centered. Romans 15:1–3 says, "Let each of us please *his* neighbor for *his* good, leading to edification. For even Christ did not please Himself; but as it is written, *'The reproaches of those who reproached You fell on Me.'*" According to 2 Corinthians 12:14–21, edification doesn't seek its own (verse 14) but is willing to love without being loved (verses 15–16).

The point: Once you choose to put off your corrupt words, you need to replace them with good words. Good words come from God who delivers the good words He wants you to say through the Holy Spirit and strengthens you to speak them. Then God uses the good words He gives you to edify the people around you.

## 2. God uses the good words He gives you to minister His grace

*". . . that it may impart grace to the hearers." (Ephesians 4:29)*

God also uses your good words to minister His grace. God's grace is an amazing force. It's "the free expression of the loving kindness of God to men, finding its only motive in the bounty and benevolence of the Giver's unearned and unmerited favor."[5] Besides saving you by grace, God uses His grace to bring joy, pleasure, gratification, favor, and acceptance into your life.[6] On top of all that, God gives you the fantastic honor of using your words to impart His grace to the people around you.

According to Paul, God's grace enriches your good words so they can accomplish more than what's humanly possible. "I thank my God always concerning you for the grace of God which was given to you by Christ Jesus, that you were enriched in everything by Him in all utterance and all knowledge" (1 Corinthians 1:4–5). This enrichment energizes your words so they can accomplish God's purposes.

Here are some ways God wants to enrich your words to achieve His purposes in people's lives.

God wants to use your words to bring comfort to the grieving. When Paul wrote to the Thessalonians about their concerns over those who died before Christ's return, he assured them they had nothing to fear. They would be reunited with their deceased loved ones when Christ returned. Paul said, "Therefore comfort one another with these words" (1 Thessalonians 4:18). Knowing what to say to a grieving person can be hard. Here are a few pointers: 1. Nothing you can say will fix the loss so don't try. Share in their grief. 2. Saying "I'm so sorry for your loss" with a hug can do amazing things. Caring words combined with appropriate touch can be very comforting. 3. Don't skip to the end of grief. When the person is in the beginning or middle of their grief and you skip to the final stage of acceptance, saying things like "He's in a better place," or "At least you don't have to clean up after him anymore" your words can be very hurtful. 4. Don't be afraid to talk with the grieving person about their deceased loved one. They're already thinking about them and it's comforting to know you are too. Like Paul, God wants to use your thoughtful words to comfort the grieving.

God wants to use your good words to enhance worship. Church services are filled with words, and you can take advantage of this time together by using good words to enhance your worship. Paul tells you in Colossians 3:16–17 that you should be participating in "teaching and admonishing one another in psalms and hymns and spiritual songs, singing with grace in your hearts to the Lord. And *whatever* you do in word or deed, *do* all in the name of the Lord Jesus, giving thanks to God the Father through Him." You can share God's word in the Psalms, give testimony of God's goodness in your life, and sing a hymn or spiritual song that teaches the essential doctrines of the church. When you express thanks to God at church, you're using good words.

As a leader, God wants to use your good words as an example to others. Paul wanted Timothy to understand the importance of leaders being an example with their words in 1 Timothy 4:12, saying, "Let no one despise your youth, but be an example to the believers in word, in conduct, in love, in spirit, in faith, in purity." When you as a leader speak the truth in love, are honest about your offenses when you hurt someone, tell others about the sins you're struggling with so they can pray for you, and speak about your hurt to the person who sins against you when appropriate, people notice. When you're honest with those who have authority over you and about your faith in Christ in the face of hostility, and do the things discussed in this chapter you lead people by example to do the same.

God wants to use your good words to validate His character. You saw in the last chapter that when you, as a child of God, say one thing and do another, you bring shame to God's name. However, according to 2 Corinthians 1:15–24, when you say what you mean, you show the world that God says what He means, and you prove that "all the promises of God in Him *are* Yes, and in Him Amen, to the glory of God through us." You have a unique opportunity to represent God to the world.

God wants to use your good words to validate your witness. When you use corrupt words one day, then invite someone to church the next, you can ruin your chances of sharing your faith with that person. On the other hand, John says your good words can combine with your good deeds to prove your witness is true. You can be like the Samaritan woman who told everyone in her village about Jesus. "And many of the Samaritans of that city believed in Him because of the word of the woman who testified, 'He told me all that I *ever* did'" (John 4:39) (see 1 Peter 3:13–17; Titus 2:7–8).

Finally, your words need to be filtered through grace. Although God enriches your words through grace, you're free to say words that bring death instead of life. You need to make sure your words are from God and not from your flesh. Paul says in Colossians 4:6, "*Let* your speech always *be* with grace, seasoned with salt, that you may know how you ought to answer each one."

There was a time early in my ministry when I was talking to someone and thought, *Wow, the things I am saying are insightful.* Later I discovered that my words hurt the person because they weren't filtered by grace. What I said may have been true, but that didn't mean I should say it. Seasoning your words with grace means you take the time to figure out when you should and shouldn't say something and whether saying something will hurt the person or help them.

The point: God enriches your good words with grace so they can accomplish His purposes. God uses good words to comfort the grieving, enhance worship, and help leaders as they lead. Your good words also prove God's character and validate your witness to the unsaved. Finally, you need to filter your words through grace so you can know how to speak to others.

## 3. God doesn't want your words to grieve the Holy Spirit

*"And do not grieve the Holy Spirit of God, by whom you were sealed for the day of redemption." (Ephesians 4:30)*

The thought that I can grieve the Holy Spirit is very sobering. The word "grieve" means to offend or afflict with sorrow.[7] There's been much speculation about what it means to grieve the Spirit. However, Paul puts this verse about grieving the Spirit in the context of your words. I believe there's specifically something about Christians using corrupt words that grieves the Spirit.

To understand how you can afflict the Spirit with sorrow or offend Him, you must look at the Spirit's job in your life and your words. As you saw in Chapter 1, when you were saved, your spirit, which was dead because of the effects of sin, was made alive by the Spirit of God (Ephesians 2:4–5). The Spirit also guarantees that you will spend forever in heaven (Ephesians 1:13–14), makes you a part of the church, which is the body of Christ on Earth (Ephesians 4:15–16), and helps you understand the Bible (1 John 2:27). The Spirit also made His home in you and indwells you (Romans 8:11). Look at what John says about the indwelling of the Holy Spirit.

> And I will pray the Father, and He will give you an-
> other Helper, that He may abide with you forever—
> the Spirit of truth, whom the world cannot receive,
> because it neither sees Him nor knows Him; but you
> know Him, for He dwells with you and will be in you
> (John 14:16–17).

According to John, the Holy Spirit lives in you from the moment you trust Christ for your forgiveness and will live inside you
even after you enter God's presence in heaven. You've already
learned in this chapter that the Holy Spirit also gives you the good
words God wants you to say when you need them (Luke 12:11; see
also Acts 4:3–11 and 1 Corinthians 2:1–16). So, how do your corrupt
words grieve the Spirit?

You may see your corrupt words as no big deal, but they're a
symptom of a much bigger problem. According to Jesus, corrupt
words come from a corrupt heart.

> For a good tree does not bear bad fruit, nor does a
> bad tree bear good fruit. For every tree is known by
> its own fruit. For men do not gather figs from thorns,
> nor do they gather grapes from a bramble bush. A
> good man out of the good treasure of his heart brings
> forth good; and an evil man out of the evil treasure of
> his heart brings forth evil. For out of the abundance
> of the heart his mouth speaks (Luke 6:43–45).

This is important. If corrupt words come out of your mouth,
you're putting them into your heart. If you listen to the same music
you listened to before you were saved, watch the same TV shows,
read the same magazines and books, and spend your time talking
with the same people, all the evil treasure you're putting into your
heart can't help but come out of your mouth. Your corrupt words

grieve the Spirit because He's living inside a Christian whose filling their heart with the filth of evil treasure. He's also grieved because He's living in a Christian whose evil heart blocks the good words God wants Him to deliver. What can you do?

You learned in Chapter 2 that to put off the old man/woman you used to be you need to do things that feed your spirit instead of the flesh. In the same way, the only way to keep from grieving the Spirit is by putting off your old way of living and replacing it with things that feed your spirit. You need to start reading the Bible, listening to Christian music, praying, going to church, and making and spending time with Christian friends. Then you'll be able to put off speaking corrupt words and put on the new way of using good words to edify and minister grace to the people around you.

The point: The Holy Spirit is afflicted with sorrow and offended by you when He's forced to live in a filthy heart that blocks Him from giving you the good words God wants you to say. To avoid grieving the Spirit with your words, you must stop filling your heart with "evil treasure" and start filling it with "good treasure."

## Conclusion

God wants you to replace the corrupt words you used before you were saved with the good words He wants to give you through His Spirit. Your good words can do more to edify the people around you than is humanly possible because God enriches them with His grace. You have an added motivation to replace your corrupt words with good words because your corrupt words grieve the Holy Spirit.

God wants you to change by:

<u>Putting off the old</u>    and    <u>Putting on the new</u>
Corrupt Words                  Good Words

Discussion Questions

1. Do you have any thoughts or questions about this chapter?

2. When has someone said something that encouraged you?

3. What are some things you would like people to say that would comfort you?

4. Where do you need to start using good words?

5. Is there someone you can say good words to this week?

6. How serious is it when you grieve the Holy Spirit?

# 11

# Put off Toxic Anger

*"Let all bitterness, wrath, anger, clamor, and evil speaking be put away from you, with all malice." (Ephesians 4:31)*

When Terry met Glen, he was ready to shut down his construction business. Glen had a falling out with his foreman and needed someone to finish the remaining jobs. Terry agreed to help and got to work as Glen's only carpenter. Once the open jobs were finished Glen invited Terry to keep working, and their temporary relationship turned into a mutually beneficial partnership. Things were going well until, without warning, Glen decided to hire Bob, a more experienced carpenter, to take over as supervisor on the job site. It was a big adjustment for Terry. He'd gone from working on his own to working for someone who was trying to prove himself. On top of that, Bob's pay was based on his productivity. The more they got done, the more Bob got paid. Bob would comment about Terry's speed and then talk about how much more money he could make if Terry worked faster.

Bob and Terry were working on a remodeling project when Terry's efforts to work faster caused him to accidentally knock over Bob's level. Levels are sensitive instruments and shouldn't be knocked around, so Terry apologized, picked up Bob's level, and put it back on the ledge. Bob gave Terry a cold stare, walked over to his level, and knocked it over. Terry was stunned to see how intentional Bob was about paying him back for accidentally knocking over his level.

The last part of your old man Paul says you need to put off to be ready for Christ to use is toxic anger. You already learned in Chapters 5 and 6 that you can "be angry" without sinning. What you may not know, is that if you don't deal with the anger you have at an offense before the sun goes down, you'll use toxic anger to punish the people who offend you. Paul lists six kinds of toxic anger in Ephesians 4:31. They are:

- Bitterness
- Wrath
- Anger
- Clamor
- Evil speaking
- Malice

I call them toxic anger languages after the five love languages Dr. Gary Chapmen discusses in his book *The Five Love Languages*. Dr. Chapman teaches that everyone has love languages they use to show and receive love. Similarly, these six toxic anger languages are what people use to show their anger when they don't deal with it properly.

You may see yourself in many of the following descriptions. However, like Dr. Chapman's five love languages, most people have a primary (the one you use most of the time) and secondary (the one you use some of the time) toxic anger language. You'll be able to discover yours by taking the quiz at the end of this chapter.

## 1. To be free of toxic anger, you need to put off bitterness

The Greek word for "bitterness" comes from the word for the gourd of a particular wild vine that's so bitter and acrid that it's "a kind of poison."[1] Like the poison gourd, bitterness is anger that poisons your mind so you can't see the good in people who offend you.

I remember talking to a friend at church about hiding plastic eggs for our upcoming Church Easter Egg hunt. I mentioned how I didn't understand how some Christians were against it when it's such a great outreach opportunity. Over the next few weeks, he started making strange comments to me. He was critical and suspicious about everything I did. I didn't know what was happening. Then I remembered a conversation we'd had years before when he told me he was offended by the pagan aspects of Easter. I realized he thought I was attacking his beliefs. He was offended but didn't say anything. Since his toxic anger language was bitterness, he started seeing only the bad in me. Once I apologized, he forgave me and could see good in me again.

Bitterness is dangerous. It starts by making you critical and suspicious of the person who hurts you. Then it grows until you can see no good in the person. If your bitterness goes unchecked, it can keep you from seeing the good in your life. But the poison of bitterness doesn't stop there. The writer of Hebrews warns you to look carefully "lest any root of bitterness springing up cause trouble, and by this many become defiled" (Hebrews 12:15). Bitterness is like a dangerous infection. Once it takes away your ability to see the grace of God in all the good things He gives you, it can spread to others.

Bitterness is a toxic tool you use to punish the person who offends you when you don't deal with your anger. The problem with bitterness is that it hurts the person with it most. Even the person responsible for creating the bitterness doesn't suffer as much. The old proverb is right when it says, "No matter how long you nurse a grudge, it won't get better."

> Describe a time when you either observed or experienced bitterness.
>
> _____
> _____
> _____
> _____
> _____

The point: When you have difficulty seeing the good in people who wrong you, you struggle with the toxic anger language of bitterness. Bitterness isn't an appropriate response to an offense because it blinds you to God's grace. You need to put off bitterness.

## 2. To be free of toxic anger, you need to put off "wrath"

Another toxic anger language is "wrath." The word "wrath" in this verse isn't the same as the *orgay* anger referred to as wrath in Chapter 5. It's the Greek word *thumos* and refers to "passion, heat, anger boiling up and soon subsiding again." While *thumos* isn't *orgay* wrath, the *Complete Word Study Dictionary New Testament* says, "*Thumos* is an outburst of *orgay* anger."[2] One way to know you have wrath is that the anger you feel at an offense is greater than the level of the offense. How does it work?

Imagine that when someone offends you, a small amount of water, the emotion of *orgidzo* anger, is poured into a cup.

The smaller the offense, the less anger it produces and the less water it puts in the cup. The greater the offense, the more anger it produces and the more water it puts in the cup.

Small Offense        Great Offense

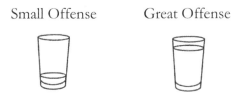

When your six-year-old daughter steals a cookie from the cookie jar, your anger level might cover the bottom of the cup.

When your 17-year-old son gets caught selling drugs, the anger might fill half or three-quarters of the cup.

The problem is that when you don't deal with your anger, it builds up, and like the water that fills the cup, it reduces your capacity to absorb new offenses. Over time, you become full of anger.

Now imagine that the point at which your cup overflows with water is when you explode and boil over into hurtful words or deeds. This is *thumos* or wrath.

If you let your anger build, eventually, even the slightest offense can cause you to explode. Then, when something as minor as your child stealing a cookie from the cookie jar happens, your anger erupts like a volcano. Fortunately, you can prevent yourself from exploding by dealing with offenses through forgiveness or transfer. When you do, the cup empties and the anger disappears.

Billy Sunday, a nineteenth-century preacher, told the story of a woman who came to him and tried to rationalize her angry outbursts. "Mr. Sunday, I know I have a bad temper, but I am over with it in a minute." "So is the shotgun," Sunday replied, "but it blows everything to pieces."[3] The person with wrath (*thumos*) needs to stop minimizing the harm it does and see it for the destructive force it is.

---

Do you struggle with wrath? Describe how:

_____

_____

_____

_____

_____

---

The point: If you blow up when you get angry, and your anger quickly subsides again, or there are times when your anger is greater than the severity of the offense, your toxic anger language is wrath (*thumos*). Wrath (*thumos*) is one of the world's ways of dealing with anger. You must put off wrath (*thumos*) if you want to live the life God intends for you.

## 3. To be free of toxic anger, you need to put off vengeance

The next toxic anger language Paul tells you to put off is *anger*. *Anger* is the Greek word "*orgay*" and is "anger exhibited in punishment, hence used for punishment itself."[4] This is one of those places where the word *orgay* is translated as anger, so to clear up the confusion, I'll use "vengeance" for the rest of this section.

You learned in chapter 5 that when the Bible talks about God's vengeance, it's describing His righteous anger or the right He has to demand payment for an injustice or an offense (Jeremiah 17:10). You also learned that you don't have the right to take vengeance because you can't search the heart or test the mind of the person who offends you. You can't even know what punishment would be appropriate for each offense. Therefore, your vengeance-based actions are always wrong.

Vengeance is what you do to actively punish the person who offends you. Vengeance is active but isn't necessarily preplanned. Sometimes you plan how to get even, but other times you may see an opportunity and don't resist it. Regardless, your goal is to inflict pain on the person who offended you. It can be as small as kicking over someone's level or as scary as hiring a hitman to kill your boss. The mantra of the person who uses vengeance is, "I don't get mad; I get even."

Frederick Buechner explained the problem of vengeance well:

> Of the 7 deadly sins, anger is possibly the most fun. To lick your wounds, to smack your lips over grievances long past, to roll over your tongue the prospect of bitter confrontations still to come, to savor to the last toothsome morsel both the pain you are given and the pain you are giving back—in many ways it is a feast fit for a king. The chief drawback is that what you are wolfing down is yourself. The skeleton at the feast is you.[5]

When someone in the Old Testament did something to offend someone, like stealing their sheep or making them lose an eye, the person could demand repayment. This is the "eye-for-an-eye" mentality. However, Jesus changed all that when He said:

> You have heard that it was said, "An eye for an eye and a tooth for a tooth." But I tell you not to resist an evil person. But whoever slaps you on your right cheek, turn the other to him also (Matthew 5:38–39).

Now, because Jesus died on the cross and offers you forgiveness by grace through faith (Ephesians 2:8), God expects you to give up your right to punish the people who offend you and forgive them just like He forgives you. When you refuse to forgive, you trample on God's forgiveness and risk what Jesus warned His disciples about in Matthew 6:14–15, "For if you forgive men their trespasses, your heavenly Father will also forgive you. But if you do not forgive men their trespasses, neither will your Father forgive your trespasses."

---

Do you struggle with vengeance? Describe how:

_____

_____

_____

_____

_____

_____

---

The point: If you punish the people who offend you by directly hurting them, your toxic anger language is vengeance. You must put off vengeance if you want to forgive others as God forgives you.

## 4. To be free of toxic anger, you need to put off clamor

Another toxic anger language is clamor. *Clamor* is a tumult or outcry that uses volume to silence the person you're angry with.[6] One of the Bible's best examples of clamor is found in Acts 23 when the Romans took Paul prisoner after being accused by the Jews of bringing a Gentile with him into the temple.

The Roman soldiers brought Paul to the chief priest and the Jewish council to answer for his actions. Paul saw that half of the council were Pharisees who believed in the resurrection of the dead and the other half were Sadducees who didn't, so he yelled out, "My brothers, I am a Pharisee, the son of a Pharisee. I stand on trial because of my hope in the resurrection of the dead" (*New International Version,* Acts 23:6). Then "there arose a loud outcry" (Acts 23:9) as both sides tried to silence the other by yelling each other down.

I've seen clamor when a mother raises her voice each time her son tries to say something she doesn't want to hear and when a husband yells at the top of his lungs at his wife so she can't voice her opinion. Clamor can be a daughter turning the music up in her room so she doesn't have to listen to her mother or a son turning on his earbuds so he doesn't have to hear his father's lecture. Whatever the form, the message of clamor is the same: "I'm not going to listen to you because I'm angry with you!"

But God says, "Do not strive with a man without cause, if he has done you no harm" (Proverbs 3:30) and, "He who answers a matter before he hears *it,* It *is* folly and shame to him" (Proverbs 18:13). Clamor is toxic because it does both things and prevents you from finding out if your anger is justified or not.

---

Do you struggle with clamor? Describe how:

_____

_____

_____

_____

_____

_____

---

The point: If you yell to silence the person you're angry with, such as your children, spouse, or employees, you're using the toxic anger language of clamor. You need to give up clamor to make sure your anger is justified and then deal with it through forgiveness or transfer.

## 5. To be free of toxic anger, you need to put off evil speaking

The fifth toxic anger language Paul names is evil speaking. *Evil speaking* is slander or speech that injures someone's good name by ruining their reputation intentionally or unintentionally.[7] Intentional evil speaking is a vicious attack to hurt the person you're angry with. It can be lies posted on Facebook to ruin someone's reputation or accusations in the break room to get someone in trouble with the boss.

On the other hand, unintentional evil speaking can be as simple as telling someone else how you've been hurt instead of going to the person who hurt you and confronting them. If you're an incidental evil speaker like me, you may say things because you need to talk about the injustice or because you want the people around you to know the person you're angry with is guilty.

You would expect evil speaking to happen at your job or school, but evil speaking is just as likely to happen in the church. Evil speaking is toxic whether it's intentional or unintentional because it injures the good name of the person you're speaking about.

---

Do you struggle with evil speaking? Describe how:

_____

_____

_____

_____

_____

_____

---

The point: Whether you want to hurt the reputation of the person you're angry with or vent about what they've done to you, you're using the toxic anger language of evil speaking. You need to put off evil speaking.

## 6. To be free of toxic anger, you need to put off malice

The last toxic anger language Paul tells you to put off is malice. *Malice* is passive maliciousness, naughtiness, or wickedness of the heart.[8] Malice is like wrath in that you punish the person who offends you, but with malice, your goal is to do it without anyone knowing. You know you're punishing the person you're angry with because you enjoy seeing them suffer.

Dave and Bob went to First Christian Church. Dave ran the church's ministry for the poor, while Bob was the church's biggest giver. One day, Dave blew up at Bob over how he treated a homeless person in his ministry. The tension lasted several months, but when Bob started talking to him again, Dave thought the conflict had blown over and everything was fine. Dave didn't know Bob started giving all his offerings to the building fund. Since their church separated its finances into a general fund and a building fund, Bob's seemingly innocent giving change eventually led to a financial crisis that forced the church to end Dave's ministry. Bob was able to punish Dave without anyone knowing.

You may be tempted to justify malice by saying your actions don't directly hurt someone, but God knows your thoughts. Anything you do to hurt the people around you breaks God's command, "Beloved, do not avenge yourselves, but *rather* give place to wrath; for it is written, '*Vengeance is Mine, I will repay,*' says the Lord" (Romans 12:19).

Do you struggle with malice? Describe how:

_____
_____
_____
_____
_____
_____

The point: When you do things indirectly to hurt the people you're angry with by using subtle tools to pay them back, you're using the toxic anger language of malice. You must put off malice because it's just as wrong as vengeance (*orgay*).

## Conclusion

If you don't deal with your anger at a particular offense before the sun goes down, you will use toxic anger to punish the person you're angry with. You can't help using your toxic anger language because when you let the sun go down on your wrath, you give the devil a foothold in your life that gives him the position of authority to say no to your attempts to stop.

Take the quiz below to find your toxic anger languages. While you may feel like you have all six toxic anger languages, most people have only two so identify the two you use most often. These are your primary and secondary toxic anger languages.

# Toxic Anger Language Quiz

Put a check beside the one(s) you struggle with the most:

I have difficulty seeing the good in people who have wronged me.
Bitterness ____

I blow up when I get angry, but then my anger quickly subsides again. There are times when the level of my anger exceeds the severity of the offense.
Wrath ____

I punish the person who offends me by getting even.
Anger (orgay), vengeance ____

I yell when I'm angry to silence the person I'm angry with.
Clamor ____

I talk to other people about the person I'm angry with because I want them to know what the person did to me.

Evil speaking ____

I don't do things directly to hurt the people I'm angry with. I use more subtle tools to pay them back.

Malice ____

When you catch yourself using your toxic anger language, recognize it as a red flag warning you that someone has offended you and deal with the offense as soon as possible to remove the devil's foothold.

God wants us to change by:

Putting off the old        and        Putting on the new
        Toxic Anger

Discussion Questions

1. Do you have any thoughts or questions about this chapter?

2. If you haven't already done so, take the Toxic Anger Language.

3. What are your primary and secondary toxic anger languages?

4. When do you use them?

5. Who are you most likely to use them against?

6. How often do you use them?

# 12

# Put on Forgiving Like God

*"And be kind to one another, tenderhearted, forgiving one another, just as God in Christ forgave you." (Ephesians 4:32)*

## 1. To forgive like God, you need to use the tool of kindness
*"And be kind to one another . . ."(Ephesians 4:32)*

No one was surprised when Larry volunteered to help with the annual Children's Christmas Program. He loved to work in his church's children's ministry setting up the rooms for the teachers, gathering the supplies, and then cleaning up every week. There was a lot to do, and Larry was excited to serve.

Larry met with Pastor Jeff, the new children's pastor, to plan the program's details. They talked about the different things the kids would do during the service, from taking the offering to the children's choir singing "Silent Night" at the end. Pastor Jeff ended the meeting by telling Larry how glad he was to have him on the team.

Larry volunteered to do everything he could. He gathered and prepared the Christmas decorations for the decorating crew and bought the battery-operated candles and supplies to make the background for the play. Later, Pastor Jeff unpacked the battery-operated candles and turned one on. He snapped at Larry, "I wanted the flickering candles. These aren't going to work!" Pastor Jeff's tone surprised Larry, but he figured Pastor Jeff was under a lot of stress, so he prayed the prayer of release and let it go. Over the next few weeks, Pastor Jeff snapped at Larry whenever things didn't go how he wanted.

Finally, Larry and a group of volunteers were working on the play's background when Pastor Jeff came and asked what they were doing. Larry told him they were painting the plywood background for the stage. Pastor Jeff gave Larry the disappointed look he'd become so familiar with and snapped, "You're using the wrong colors. You need to start all over again and paint the plywood white." Then he walked away. Larry enjoyed working with the children's ministry but wasn't enjoying Pastor Jeff's temper. He could see the other volunteers felt the same way. Larry knew he needed to say something to Pastor Jeff.

During their next planning meeting, Pastor Jeff talked about how stressed he was. Larry thought *This is the perfect time to tell pastor Jeff how I feel.* He turned to Pastor Jeff and calmly said, "I know you're stressed. You've been snapping at us for weeks." Pastor Jeff's mouth opened, but nothing came out. After a few seconds, he said, "You're right, Larry. I've let my stress affect the way I've treated you and the rest of the team. I'm sorry for my sharpness, and I promise to work at stopping." Larry accepted Pastor Jeff's apology and told him he forgave him.

The next day, as the team was finishing the background, Pastor Jeff asked if he could talk to them. He said, "I need to apologize for being impatient and snapping at all of you. I'm sorry. Please forgive me." Everyone joined together and said, "I forgive you!" Then he asked if they would help keep him accountable by telling him when he slipped up again. Pastor Jeff's behavior changed over the next few weeks, and to everyone's relief, he was more patient and kinder to them.

Fortunately, you don't have to use toxic anger to punish the people who offend you. You can use the godly tools Paul talks about in Ephesians 4:32. The first tool Paul says you should use when someone offends you is kindness. The Greek word for "kindness" means "good, gentle, [and] easy to use or bear, like Christ's yoke that has nothing harsh or galling about it. It is used to describe wine that is better for drinking and food that is good for eating."[1] The word "kindness" is translated as "goodness" in Romans 2:4, where Paul says, "that the goodness of God leads you to repentance."

Jesus demonstrated kindness when He and His disciples were in Capernaum. Peter ran into a couple of temple tax collectors who asked him if Jesus paid the temple tax and he said yes. While we don't know why Peter did this, we know how Jesus handled it.

> And when he had come into the house, Jesus antici-pated him, saying, "What do you think, Simon? From whom do the kings of the earth take customs or tax-es, from their sons or from strangers?" Peter said to Him, "From strangers." Jesus said to him, "Then the sons are free. Nevertheless, lest we offend them, go to the sea, cast in a hook, and take the fish that comes up first. And when you have opened its mouth, you will find a piece of money; take that and give it to them for Me and you." Matthew 17:24–27

Look at how kind Jesus was as He dealt with Peter's offense. He didn't even confront him. He just used it as a teaching opportuni-ty and accepted the conscquences of Peter's actions. Many offenses committed against you are minor, or the results aren't significant. A "kind" response treats the person with gentleness. Larry's decision to release Pastor Jeff's first offense of snapping at him is an excellent example of kindness. Then if there's a need to confront, kindness deals with it in a way that's easy for the offending person to bear.

The point: You don't have to use toxic anger with the people who offend you. You can choose to show kindness. Kindness takes the gentlest approach possible when dealing with the person who offends you.

## 2. To forgive like God, you need to use the tool of tender-heartedness

"... tenderhearted." (Ephesians 4:32)

Tenderheartedness is another tool you should use when you deal with offenses. The word "tenderhearted" comes from the Greeks word *eú,* which means "well," and *splágchnon* meaning "bowels." It literally means well-boweled or well-boweledness. It's being "full of compassion and pity."[2]

Tenderheartedness keeps you from losing sight of your sinfulness and, therefore, able to show compassion when you deal with the sins of others. A great example of tenderheartedness is in Acts 9:10–18 when Jesus came to Ananias in a vision and told him to go to Saul and lay hands on him to give him his sight back. The only problem was that Saul hated and killed Christians. Ananias may have even known someone whom Saul killed. Still, Ananias went to Saul and restored his sight. Ananias had to recognize that he was no better than Saul and that his past sins were just as offensive to God as Saul's before he could go to him.

If Ananias could call the murderer Saul "brother" and heal his blindness, you can be tenderhearted to your spouse, children, coworkers, and neighbors. You show tenderheartedness when you show compassion to the person who hurts you because you recognize that you also have hurt others.

The point: Along with kindness, you should show tenderheartedness to the person who offends you. Tenderheartedness is never losing sight of your past sin and guilt when you deal with the sins of others.

## 3. To forgive like God, you need to use the tool of remitting

*". . . forgiving one another . . ." (Ephesians 4:32)*

The last tool Paul talks about for dealing with offenses is forgiveness. Forgiveness is what makes kindness and tenderheartedness possible. The word translated as "forgive" is *charízomai* and comes from the word *cháris* or grace. The word forgiveness has two meanings. The first one is pardoning through graciously remitting a person's sin. The second, discussed in the next section, is "handing someone over to someone."[3]

When someone offends you by sinning against you, that person owes you for the pain they caused. Forgiveness is a decision to graciously remit a person's sin by releasing the person from the debt they owe you. When someone sins against you and says, "I'm sorry," and you say, "I forgive you," you are graciously remitting their sin. When you do this, it takes away the spiritual wound and relational barrier the offense caused.

According to Luke 17:3, this kind of forgiveness depends on the repentance of the person who offended you. "Take heed to yourselves. If your brother sins against you, rebuke him; and if he repents, forgive him." You can only forgive a person by graciously remitting their sin if they first look with abhorrence at what they did, heartily amend their behavior, and then offer a sincere apology. A sincere apology happens when a person admits to committing the offense, acknowledges it was wrong, and then asks for forgiveness. The prodigal son sincerely apologized in Luke 15:21, saying, "Father, I have sinned against heaven and in your sight, and am no longer worthy to be called your son." A sincere apology can be as simple as saying, "Yes, Jerry, I did lie to you about being sick. It was wrong, and I'm sorry. Will you forgive me?"

Unfortunately, not all apologies are the same. You may have seen celebrities apologize on TV. Some are sincere, but others are simply doing damage control to help their image. Insincere apologies may sound like this: "I'm sorry you were hurt," "I'm sorry if I offended you," and "I'm sorry things happened the way they did." When you apologize, avoid words that deny your guilt. One rule of thumb is to avoid using "but" and "if" in your apologies—the words "but" or "if" can turn a sincere apology into an excuse.

> How have good or bad apologies affected your relationships in
> the past? What does a good apology do?
>
> _____
>
> _____
>
> What does a bad apology do?
>
> _____
>
> _____

Once a person offers a sincere apology, you should forgive
them, say, "I forgive you," and then reaffirm your love for them.
Your words are important, so you should say, "I forgive you." Here
are some examples to avoid: "That's okay," "Forget it," "It's no big
deal," or saying nothing at all.

> Tip: It's just as important for the person who offended you to
> hear "I forgive you" as it is for you to hear "I am sorry" to restore
> the relationship and remove the break that was caused by the of-
> fense.

You may wonder, "Is it that important to forgive someone?"
Jesus says in Matthew 6:14–15 that forgiveness isn't optional. "For if
you forgive men their trespasses, your heavenly Father will also forgive you. But if you do not forgive men their trespasses, neither will
your Father forgive your trespasses." Unforgiveness shows a lack of
true repentance. You may think you're a godly person who obeys
God because you go to church and read your Bible, but God says
obedience starts with forgiveness. If you don't forgive others for the
sins they commit against you, you aren't truly repentant for the sins
you commit against God. Forgiveness and repentance go hand in
hand.

It's also important to remember that everyone has a forgiveness tempo. Some people forgive quickly, while others forgive

more slowly. God doesn't tell you how soon you should say, "I forgive you," except that it must be before sunset. Remember, however, if you wait too long, you give the devil a foothold in your life and risk becoming a tool Satan can use to hurt the person God brought to repentance. "So that, on the contrary, you *ought* rather to forgive and comfort *him,* lest perhaps such a one be swallowed up with too much sorrow. . . lest Satan should take advantage of us; for we are not ignorant of his devices" (2 Corinthians 2:7, 11). Forgive as quickly as possible.

Someone once asked me, "What if the person's done the same thing before? Can the person truly be repentant?" Yes! If someone sincerely apologizes, you should forgive the person again. That's why Jesus says in Luke 17:4, "And if he sins against you seven times in a day, and seven times in a day returns to you, saying, 'I repent,' you shall forgive him." Make Andrew Murray's prayer your own.

To forgive like *You,* blessed Son of God!
I take this as the law of my life.
*You* who *have* given the command, *give* also the power.
*You* who *had* love enough to forgive me, *will* also fill
me with love and teach me to forgive others.
*You* who *did* give me the first blessings, in the joy of
having my sins forgiven, *will* surely give me
the second blessing, and deeper joy of forgiving others as You *have* forgiven me.
Oh, fill me with the faith in the power of *Your* love in
me, to make me like *Yourself,* to enable me to
forgive the seventy times seven, and so to
love and bless all around me.

O My Jesus, *Your* example is my law:
I must be like *You.*
And *Your* example is my gospel too.
I can be as *You are.*

*You are* at once my law and my life.

What *You demand* of me by *Your* example, *You work* in
    me by *Your* life.

I shall forgive like *You*.

Lord, only lead me deeper into my dependence on
    *You*, into all sufficiency of *Your* grace and the
    blessed keeping which comes from *Your* in-
    dwelling.

Then *will* I believe and prove the all-prevailing power
    of love.

I *will* forgive even as Christ has forgiven me. Amen.[4]

The point: You can show forgiveness if you graciously remit the sin of someone who apologizes for their offense. For an apology to work, it must be sincere. When you receive a sincere apology, you should always forgive the person who offended you.

## 4. To forgive like God, you need to use the transfer tool

*" . . . forgiving one another, just as God in Christ forgave you." (Ephesians 4:32)*

The second meaning of "forgive" is "handing something over to someone."[5] When the Jewish leaders accused the Apostle Paul of bringing a Gentile into the Temple at Jerusalem, the governor considered turning Paul over to them so he could stand trial. But Paul said, "No one can deliver [*charízomai*] me to them. I appeal to Caesar" (Acts 25:11).

Paul knew the Jewish leaders would kill him if he were handed over, so he made an appeal as a Roman citizen that kept him out of their hands. This "handing something over to someone"[6] is the imprecatory prayer of transfer you've already learned about in Chapter 6. It includes:

1. Naming the offense and the person who committed it.
2. Acknowledging the anger, pain, and injury the offense produced.
3. Declaring your transfer of the right of vengeance to God.

If you pray from a sincere heart and make a genuine decision to transfer an offense to God, transfer frees you from the anger and pain of the offense. Then you can be loving to the person who offended you and do what Paul says in Romans 12:20–21 even though you haven't received an apology.

> Therefore, "If your enemy is hungry, feed him; If he is thirsty, give him a drink; For in so doing you will heap coals of fire on his head." Do not be overcome by evil, but overcome evil with good.

The best way to know you've dealt with an offense properly is by how you treat the person who offended you, because you can't be loving toward someone you are angry with. You can be polite, even nice, but you can't be loving. God did this same thing for you when He took His wrath toward you and transferred it to Jesus on the cross. That's why John says:

> Beloved, let us love one another, for love is of God; and everyone who loves is born of God and knows God. He who does not love does not know God, for God is love. In this the love of God was manifested toward us, that God has sent His only begotten Son into the world, that we might live through Him. In this is love, not that we loved God, but that He loved us and sent His Son to be the propitiation for our

sins. Beloved, if God so loved us, we also ought to love one another (1 John 4:7–11).

The point: You can forgive like God by graciously remitting the sin of someone who sincerely apologizes for their offense or by turning them and their offense over to God with an imprecatory prayer of transfer. Transfer is the next step in dealing with offenses when graciously remitting isn't possible.

## Conclusion

God wants you to give up using toxic anger to deal with offenses. You need to start dealing with offenses by using the tools of kindness, tenderheartedness, and forgiveness through remitting and releasing.

God wants you to change by:

<u>Putting off the old</u>    and    <u>Putting on the new</u>
Toxic Anger                Forgiving Like God

Discussion Questions

1. Do you have any thoughts or questions about this chapter?

2. Where would you rate yourself as a forgiver? Explain.

Slow                      Fast

1     2     3     4     5

3. When have you had to apologize to someone?

4. How would other people rate your apologies?

     Insincere               Sincere

        1      2      3      4      5

5. What do you say when someone says, "I'm sorry"?

6. To whom could you apologize or offer forgiveness?

# 13

# Dealing with Long-Term Offenses

*"And be kind to one another, tenderhearted, forgiving one another, just as God in Christ forgave you." (Ephesians 4:32)*

## 1. To forgive like God, you need to deal with the problem of long-term offenses

When Mary came to me for counseling, her panic attacks, which started a few months earlier, were growing in frequency and intensity. I taught her coping skills used for panic attacks, but they weren't helping. Fortunately, I was going to a pastors' conference where I hoped to get advice on how to help Mary. I went to a session led by Dr. Gary Chapman, nationally known counselor and author of the book *The Five Love Languages,* and thought, *Surely Dr. Chapman can give me advice about how to help Mary.* After the session, I went and explained Mary's problem. He told me to read his book *The Other Side of Love* and complete the process he described for dealing with long-term offenses.

I bought the book and studied the process. I learned that Mary's panic attacks were caused by the pain she carried from the many offenses she'd suffered throughout her life but never dealt with. Dr. Chapman assured me that once she completed the process, she would be free of the pain causing the attacks, and the attacks would subside. Here's the process Dr. Chapman describes in his book.

Begin with your earliest memories; focus on your childhood, your relationships with your mother, father, and brother. If all of them wronged you at one time or another, which would be pretty normal, list their names and list the ways in which they wronged you. Be specific when you have specific memories. For example, if your brother hit you over the head with a ball bat, put it down: "Ned hit me with a bat when I was ten." Be as specific and detailed as you can.[1]

I couldn't ask Mary to go through the process without knowing how it worked, so I decided to try it on myself first. I didn't know why, but I put it off for weeks. Eventually, with our next counseling session just days away, I listed every offense I could remember. I can't tell you how hard it was. I wrote pages of offenses with years of hurt from childhood through adulthood. Then I prayed the Prayer of Release for each one. It felt like God was pulling weeds from my heart, but the relief I felt afterward was amazing. Even more amazing was how the painful memories that plagued my mind for years started fading away. Soon I felt no pain from them at all.

I started to work with Mary in our next session. We took several weeks to work through all her anger and pain. Dr. Chapman was right. When we were done, Mary's panic attacks went away. Like Gulliver, held down by so many tiny ropes on the island of Lilliput, Mary's lifetime of offenses gave the devil a foothold and kept her from finding relief from her panic attacks. Once Mary released the offenses, the Devil's foothold was removed, and she was freed. Panic attacks are just one way the Devil's foothold can affect you. The Devil's foothold can also keep you from using the three godly tools of kindness, tenderheartedness, and forgiveness talked about in Chapter 12. Fortunately, Dr. Chapman's process for releasing long-term offenses can help.[2]

How does it work? One of the side effects of not dealing with an offense is that you keep a clear memory of it indefinitely. Fresh feelings of pain or anger are often brought to the surface when you think about or are forced to remember an offense. While this is a negative consequence of unforgiveness, it's also a continuous call from God to deal with these offenses. God allows painful memories to remain intact and within easy mental reach so you can deal with the offenses that caused them.

The point: To use the godly tools of kindness, tenderheartedness, and forgiveness, you need to be free of your anger from long-term offenses. Dr. Chapman gave you a process to do just that.

## 2. To forgive like God, you need to overcome the obstacles that are keeping you from dealing with long-term offenses

One obstacle that can keep you from dealing with your long-term offenses is the problem of suffering. You might struggle with transferring offenses to God because you blame Him for allowing you to suffer in the first place. Honestly, I've questioned why God allows suffering. I remember thinking at one tough time in my life, *Either God is powerful enough to prevent suffering but doesn't care, or He cares but isn't powerful enough to prevent it.* I knew I was wrong, but I couldn't understand why a good God would allow disease, death, and suffering.

Eventually, I understood that suffering is the consequence of Adam's sin. When Adam sinned, he brought death and suffering into the world. "Therefore, just as through one man sin entered the world, and death through sin, and thus death spread to all men, because all sinned" (Romans 5:12). Romans 8:20–22 says that even the physical world suffers because of Adam's sin.

> For the creation was subjected to futility, not willingly, but because of Him who subjected it in hope; because the creation itself also will be delivered from the bondage of corruption into the glorious liberty of the children of God. For we know that the whole creation groans and labors with birth pangs together until now.

Earthquakes, tsunamis, hurricanes, fires, tornados, animal attacks, disease, and meteorite strikes all happen because Adam sinned.

Fortunately, God had a plan for removing the effects of Adam's sin before he even committed it. Paul explains how in Romans 5:19, saying, "For as by one man's disobedience many were made sinners, so also by one Man's obedience many will be made righteous." God's plan for defeating the consequences of sin and suffering is called redemption. The word redemption means freeing captives by paying a ransom for them.[3]

Redemption is possible because Jesus, the "one Man," paid our ransom by suffering and dying on the cross for our sins and rising again. Now God is saving as many people as possible from the lake of fire so they can be with Him in Heaven. Eventually, the day will come when the consequences of Adam's sin will be undone. "For the earnest expectation of the creation eagerly waits for the revealing of the sons of God" (Romans 8:19).

Unfortunately, Christians aren't excused from suffering. We must live with the reality of suffering while waiting for God to finish His work. Paul talked about the suffering he endured in 2 Corinthians 11:23–27.

> In stripes above measure, in prisons more frequently, in deaths often. From the Jews five times I received forty stripes minus one. Three times I was beaten with rods; once I was stoned; three times I was shipwrecked; a night and a day I have been in the deep; in journeys often, in perils of waters, in perils of robbers, in perils of my own countrymen, in perils of the Gentiles, in perils in the city, in perils in the wilderness, in perils in the sea, in perils among false brethren; in weariness and toil, in sleeplessness often, in hunger and thirst, in fastings often, in cold and nakedness.

Paul suffered more than most people, but he was willing to endure suffering, saying, "For I consider that the sufferings of this present time are not worthy to be compared with the glory which shall be revealed in us" (Romans 8:18). As long as this world exists suffering will be a part of it. Still, God promises that one day there will be a new Heaven and Earth where pain has passed away:

> . . . . for the first heaven and the first earth had passed away . . . And God will wipe away every tear from their eyes; there shall be no more death, nor sorrow, nor crying. There shall be no more pain, for the former things have passed away (Revelation 21:1,4).

But for now, God promises to use your suffering for your benefit while you're here on Earth. "And we know that all things work together for good to those who love God, to those who are the called according to His purpose" (Romans 8:28). I've seen God use suffering in my life to open my eyes to my sin and my need for Him, to understand the suffering of others better so He can use me to comfort them, and to remind me that "our light affliction, which is but for a moment, is working for us a far more exceeding *and* eternal weight of glory (2 Corinthians 4:17). Whatever the reason, you can trust that God will use suffering for your good. If you complete the process of dealing with your long-term offenses, God will work His good by healing you of the pain of those events.

Another obstacle that can keep you from dealing with your long-term offenses is the foothold of Satan. I didn't realize it, but Satan was working to keep me from going through the process when I was trying to deal with my long-term offenses. He used every trick he could to keep me from getting started.

One of Satan's most powerful weapons is unforgiveness because it gives him a position of authority in your life (Ephesians 4:26–27; 2 Corinthians 2:6–11), and he won't give it up easily. Nevertheless, Paul says in 2 Corinthians 10:3–5 that you have spiritual weapons to defeat Satan's strongholds. Two of your most powerful spiritual weapons are prayer and forgiveness.

If you claim God's promise in James 4:7 and submit to Him, resisting whatever schemes Satan might be using, God will give you the strength to remove the Devil's foothold in your life.

The point: You have a lifetime of offenses that are giving Satan a foothold in your life. Dr. Gary Chapman gives you a process to deal with long-term offenses through releasing. You need to overcome the obstacles of suffering and Satan's opposition to be freed from the pain of past offenses.

## 3. To forgive like God, you need to carry out the process of overcoming long-term offenses

There are two ways to deal with long-term offenses. The first way is to enlist the help of a trusted spiritual mentor or pastor who can take you through the interview pages in the next chapter. Ask them to get a copy of this book and read chapters 5–6 and 10–13. Then schedule a meeting with your mentor to work through the "With Help" section that starts on the next page.

The other option is to go through the process on your own. It's possible to go through the interview pages in the next chapter alone, but sometimes identifying offenses is easier when you have help. Also, if you've suffered from traumatic events such as sexual abuse, I strongly suggest getting help. However, if you decide to go through the interview independently, skip to the "On Your Own" section on page 162.

> WARNING
> PTSD is a condition that should only be treated by people who have proper psychological training. This tool is not intended as a treatment for PTSD.

# With Help

## Find a Good Helper

What does a good helper look like? A helper needs to be:

- Emotionally healthy: There are many who, because of the pain in their lives, want to help others find emotional healing. Those who find healing from their own painful experiences and want to minister to others with similar experiences can help with little risk of hurting the person they're trying to help. However, those who try to minister to others without finding personal healing from their pain have a greater risk of causing harm. Make sure the person you ask has found healing from their pain before they try to help you.

- Spiritually mature: The Bible consistently talks about the importance of spiritual maturity and gives many qualities that a spiritually mature person possesses. Here's a list of some of those qualities:
  - ➤ They've been saved for a reasonable length of time
  - ➤ They read the Bible, pray, and attend church regularly
  - ➤ They don't gossip about others
  - ➤ They've put off sins like lying, abusing anger, stealing, using corrupt words, toxic anger, etc.
  - ➤ The church respects them as a mature Christian
  
  (While these qualities don't guarantee spiritual maturity, they provide a good framework for assessing it.)

- Compassionate: A good helper can empathize, recognize, and understand your pain. This is an important quality. Sometimes I'll stop and have the person release a particularly painful offense because I don't want them to wait until the end of the 40 minutes to release it. A good helper must be sensitive enough to see this need.

- Caring: A good helper cares about your well-being. They must be more concerned with getting you through the

process with as little emotional difficulty as possible rather than just finishing the task.

- Trustworthy: The person you choose should have a
trustworthy reputation and be able to keep anything they
hear confidential. If you share your painful experiences
with someone, the last thing you need is for them to talk
to others about them.
- Respected: A helper needs to have a respected reputation
in your church community. Many people see themselves
as emotionally healthy, spiritually mature, compassionate,
caring, and trustworthy but aren't respected by others.
The only way to know for sure is to ask for outside advice.

If you don't know anyone who meets these qualifications, ask
a pastor or fellow church member for recommendations. Then
prayerfully invite the potential helper to join you in the process.

## Make a Plan with Your Helper

- Start with prayer: Ask your trusted spiritual men-
tor/pastor to pray for God to:
  - ➤ Protect you against any schemes Satan might use to
keep you from completing the process.
  - ➤ Find the courage to face the pain of your past.
  - ➤ Bring the things God wants you to deal with to mind.
  Remember, this is a spiritual battle; you must use spiritual
weapons.
- Make a plan: Schedule a time with your trusted spiritual
mentor/pastor to work on your Offense List. Since this
can be emotionally draining, you need to limit your time
to an hour per session—40 minutes for listing offenses
and 20 minutes for releasing. Print copies of the Prayer of
Release and extra list pages from Appendix E. Make sure
the location where you'll discuss your offenses is private

and peaceful. Going to Starbucks or McDonald's or having kids running around isn't conducive to making your list.

- Execute your plan: Bring your book, the Prayer of Release, and extra list pages with you and go to your planned place. Your trusted spiritual mentor/pastor should start in prayer, asking God to give you the strength and courage to work through your Offense List and bring to mind the things He wants you to release. Bring a timer or clock. Set it for 40 minutes.

- Make your list: As your spiritual mentor/pastor takes you through the interview in the next chapter, think through each question. See if any memories come to mind. If you have any memories, write them down. Here's a list of key points to remember.

  ➤ Be specific. "If your brother hit you over the head with a baseball bat, write down, 'Ned hit me with a ball bat when I was ten.'"[4]

  ➤ If there are multiple offenses in an incident, write down each offense. If you have numerous memories about the same person, write each one down separately.

  ➤ If you only have a general memory, like your brother was always picking on you, then list the general memory, "Bob always picked on me." If you have both specific and general memories about the same offense, list both.

  ➤ If memories come up for someone after you've already finished, you can go back and write them down. Just be sure to go back and release them when you pray.

  ➤ You can write on additional pages if you run out of room on a page. Use as many pages as you need.

- Pray for each offense: When the timer goes off, pray the Prayer of Release for each offense you listed. When you're done releasing, fill in the date for the items you released.
- Schedule another time: If you haven't finished the process, plan another time to continue. Give yourself time to recover between sessions. This process can be emotionally draining. Schedule as many sessions as necessary to complete the process.

## Notes for the Helper

The goal of the helper is to guide an individual through the Offense List process created by Dr. Gary Chapman.[5] You need to read chapters 5–6 and 11–14 of this book before proceeding. Here are some essential guidelines.

- Follow the person's lead
  - ➢ Let the person set/determine your role. I give people the choice of sharing their stories with me or just having me ask the interview questions. They may not know what they prefer, but you'll likely know after you ask the first question.
  - ➢ Let the person set the tempo. Some people must tell the whole story. Listening closely is essential because the offenses are often hidden within the story, and the person may be unaware of what they are. Note each offense as you hear it, then list them for the person when they finish the story. Others go directly to the offenses.
- Identify offenses
  - ➢ Understand what an offense is: An offense is a real action done by someone else that hurts the person. It can be either general or specific, but it's usually concrete. Don't try to define it with an abstract label. Be specific. "If your brother hit you over the head with a

baseball bat, write down, 'Ned hit me with a ball bat when I was ten.'"[6] It can also be justified or unjustified, but for the sake of releasing distinguishing between the two is unnecessary.

➢ Identify the offenses: It's easy to get caught up in the injustice of the offenses you're hearing, but your job is to help identify the offenses for the person you're helping.

➢ Listen carefully to each story: Multiple offenses can be woven throughout a story. If a particular event involves multiple offenses, the person won't get relief from the pain of the event until all the offenses are released. The better you identify each offense in a multiple-offense situation, the greater the healing the person will receive.

➢ Take your time: Don't push the person through the interview. Give them time to think and tell their stories. When there's a long pause, you can ask, "Is there anything else?" If they so no, then move on.

• Follow the plan

➢ Use the interview pages in Chapter 14 of this book. The interview is designed to be as thorough as possible.

➢ Stick to the schedule: Try to gauge your progress through the interview with the time left. Allot forty minutes for listing offenses and twenty minutes for releasing. It's better to end the interview a few minutes early than to move on to a new subject that will prolong the session. You may be tempted to go longer, especially if the person seems close to finishing the process. Don't do it. You don't know when you'll come across a subject with many offenses tied to it.

- Take the Helper's Challenge: I was introduced to Dr. Chapman's Long-Term Offense Process while counseling a young woman with panic attacks.[7] I took her through the process, and she was delivered from her panic attacks. However, I knew I needed to go through the process myself before I took her through it. I did, and it changed my life. If someone asks you to be a helper, I challenge you to go through the process yourself first. You aren't required to, but it will help you understand how the process works and you'll benefit significantly from it if you do.

## On Your Own

If you're going through the Offense List process on your own, here are a few tips:

- Start with prayer: Enlist someone to pray for you as you prepare to work through your Offense List. Ask them to pray for God to:
  - ➢ Protect you from any schemes Satan might use to keep you from completing the process.
  - ➢ Give you the courage to face the pain of your past.
  - ➢ Bring the things He wants you to deal with to mind.
  Remember, this is a spiritual battle; you must use spiritual weapons.
- Make a plan: Schedule a time to work on your Offense List. Since you're doing it alone, limit your time to 45 minutes because this can be emotionally draining. Let your prayer partner know when you're going to start. Ask them to pray for you while you're working on your list. Print copies of the Prayer of Release and extra list pages from Appendix E. Make sure the location you chose is private and peaceful. Going to Starbucks or McDonald's

or having kids running around isn't conducive to making your list.

- Execute your plan: Bring your book, the Prayer of Release, and extra list pages with you and go to your planned place. Start in prayer. Ask God to help you by giving you the strength and courage to work through your Offense List. Ask Him to bring the things He wants you to release to mind. Bring a timer. Set it for 30 minutes. Limit your list time to 30 minutes and 15 minutes to pray the Prayer of Release for each offense. Don't underestimate the emotional drain of working through your Offense List.

- Make your list: As you read through the interview in Chapter 14 and make your list, take time to think through each question. See if any memories come to mind. If you have any memories, write them down. Here's a list of key points to remember.

  - ➢ Be specific. "If your brother hit you over the head with a baseball bat, write down: 'Ned hit me with a ball bat when I was ten.'"[8]

  - ➢ If there are multiple offenses for an incident, write down each offense. If you have multiple memories about the same person, write each one down separately.

  - ➢ If you only have a general memory, like your brother was always picking on you, then list the general memory, "Bob always picked on me." If you have both specific and general memories about the same offense, list both.

  - ➢ If memories come up for someone you've already finished, you can go back and write them down. Just be sure to go back and release them when you pray.

  - ➢ If you run out of room on a page, you can write it on another page. Use as many pages as you need.

- When the timer goes off, pray the Prayer of Release for all the offenses you listed. When you're done releasing, fill in the date for the items you released.
- Schedule another time: If you haven't finished the process, plan another time to continue. Give yourself time to recover between sessions because this process can be emotionally draining. Schedule as many sessions as necessary to complete the process.

The point: You can deal with your long-term offenses by following a clear plan. You can go through the process with help or on your own. I encourage getting help if you've faced significant trauma or abuse. A good plan starts with prayer, is well thought out, uses adequate preparation, and schedules specific times and days.

## Conclusion

God wants you to be freed from the devil's foothold. The long-term offense process created by Dr. Gary Chapman is a tool that can help you accomplish this. You can complete the long-term offense process by using the interview in the next chapter to create your Long-term Offense List.

Discussion Questions

1. Do you have any thoughts or questions about this chapter?

2. Where would be a good place to do your Long-term Offense List?

3. When would be a good time to complete your Long-term Offense List?

4. Whom could you ask to be a helper?

5. What is the biggest obstacle keeping you from making a plan?

6. How are you going to start?

# 14

# The Long-Term Offenses Interview

As you begin your Long-Term Offense List, you'll see an Interview page with questions on the left and a lined List page on the right to write the offenses. You can start with your immediate family relationships or jump to a subject that covers something that's bothering you. However, I encourage you to take time to complete the whole interview process. Write down what the person did that hurt you. Be specific and list items separately. For example, if your brother yelled at you one time and hit you another time, write, "John yelled at me" on one line and "John hit me" on the following line. You can use more than one line for an item if necessary. Leave the far-right column "Release Date" blank. After you release the offense, you will fill in the "Release Date" section.

Ensure you have extra list pages, a timer, and a copy of the Prayer of Release. Set the timer (30 minutes if you're working alone, 40 minutes if you're working with a helper) and work on your list. When the timer goes off, pray the Prayer of Release for each item. Avoid grouping offenses together. Pray the Prayer of Release for each item separately. Continue this process until you complete your list.

When ready, begin The Offense List Interview on the next page.

# The Offense List Interview

## *Your Immediate Family Relationships*

### Mother/Stepmother

Write your mother/stepmother's name in the left column under "People." If you had more than one mother, stepmother(s), or other adult women in your home, you'll need to go through the process for each one. Now, think back to your earliest memories of childhood. Do you have any vivid, unpleasant, or painful memories of your mother/stepmother/adult women in your home, on vacations, at parties, etc.? If anything comes to mind, write it down on the opposite page under the column "Ways They Wronged Me." Take your time and think through all the memories you have from your early childhood. Write them down.

Move into your school years. Do you have any memories of your mother/stepmother/adult women from grade school/middle school? Do any memories come to mind? Write them down. Think of your high school years. Do you have any unpleasant memories of your mother/stepmother/adult women from your time in high school? If they're negative in any way, write them down. Do you have any vivid memories between high school and today? Write them down.

Take time now to see if you have any other vivid, unpleasant, or painful memories of your mother/stepmother/adult women. If you do, then write them down. If something comes to mind later, you can come back and write it down.

### Father/Stepfather

Write your father/stepfather's name in the "People" column. If you had more than one father, stepfather(s), or other adult men in your home, you'll need to go through the process for each one. Think back to your earliest memories of childhood.

| People: | Ways They Wronged Me: | Release Date |
|---|---|---|
| | | |

Do you have any vivid, unpleasant, or painful memories of your father/stepfather/adult men, at home, on vacations, at parties, etc.? If anything comes to mind, write it down.

Move into your school years. Do you have any memories of your father/stepfather/adult men from when you were in grade school? If you do, then write them down.

How about middle school? Do any memories come to mind? Write them down. Think of your high school years. Do you have any unpleasant memories of your father/stepfather/adult men from your time in high school? Write them down.

Do you have any unpleasant memories between high school and today? Write them down.

Take time now to see if you have any other vivid, unpleasant, or painful memories of your father/stepfather/adult men. If you do, then write them down. If something comes to mind later, you can come back and write it down then.

If the timer has gone off, stop and pray through each item with the Prayer of Release. Write the date in the right column under "Release Date" when you're done praying. Schedule another time to continue and let your prayer partner know.

## Siblings/Stepsiblings

Now think of your siblings, stepsiblings, or other children in your home growing up. Think back to your earliest memories of childhood. Do you have any vivid, unpleasant, or painful memories of your siblings/stepsiblings/other children, at home, on vacations, at parties, etc.? If anything comes to mind, write their names and what they did to you. You can jump from one to the other. If you didn't have any siblings or other children in your home, move on to the next section.

Do you have any memories of your siblings/stepsiblings/other children from when you were in grade school? If you do, then write them down.

How about middle school? Do any memories come to mind? If they do, write them down.

| People: | Ways They Wronged Me: | Release Date |
|---|---|---|
| | | |
| | | |
| | | |
| | | |
| | | |
| | | |
| | | |
| | | |
| | | |
| | | |
| | | |
| | | |
| | | |
| | | |
| | | |
| | | |
| | | |
| | | |
| | | |
| | | |
| | | |
| | | |
| | | |
| | | |
| | | |
| | | |
| | | |
| | | |
| | | |

Think of your high school years. Do you have any unpleasant memories of your siblings/stepsiblings/other children from your time in high school? Write them down.

Do you have any unpleasant memories between high school and today? Write them down.

Take time now to see if you have any other vivid, unpleasant, or painful memories of your siblings/stepsiblings/other children. If you do, write them down. If something comes to mind later, you can come back and write it down then. Complete this process for each of your siblings/stepsiblings/other children.

## *Your Extended Family Relationships*

### Grandparents

Now think of your extended family. Think back to your earliest memories of childhood. Do you have any vivid, unpleasant, or painful memories of your grandparents at home, on vacations, at parties, etc.? If anything comes to mind, write their names and what they did to you. You can jump from one to the other.

Move into your school years. Do you have any memories of your grandparents from when you were in grade school? If you do, write them down.

How about middle school? Do any memories come to mind? If they do, then write them down. Think of your high school years. Do you have any unpleasant memories of your grandparents from your time in high school? Write them down.

Do you have any unpleasant memories between high school and today? Write them down.

Take time now to see if you have any other vivid, unpleasant, or painful memories of your grandparents. If you do, write them down. If something comes to mind later, you can come back and write it down then. Do this for each of your grandparents.

| People: | Ways They Wronged Me: | Release Date |
|---|---|---|
| | | |

## Aunts, Uncles, and Cousins

Now think of your aunts, uncles, and cousins. Think back to your earliest memories of childhood. Do you have any vivid, unpleasant, or painful memories of your aunts, uncles, and cousins at home, on vacations, at parties, etc.?

If anything comes to mind, write their names and what they did to you. You can jump from one to the other. If you don't have any aunts, uncles, or cousins, go on to the next section.

Move into your school years. Do you have any memories of your aunts, uncles, and cousins from when you were in grade school? If you do, then write them down.

How about middle school? Do any memories come to mind? If they do, write them down.

Think of your high school years. Do you have any unpleasant memories of your aunts, uncles, and cousins from your time in high school? Write them down.

Do you have any unpleasant memories between high school and today? Write them down.

Take time now to see if you have any other vivid, unpleasant, or painful memories of your aunts, uncles, and cousins. If you do, write them down. If something comes to mind later, you can come back and write it down then. Do this for each of your aunts, uncles, and cousins.

## Your School Career

Now think of your school career. Think back to grade school. Do you have any vivid, unpleasant, or painful memories of your teachers, fellow students, or other school employees? If anything comes to mind, write their names and what they did to you. You can jump from one to the other.

Move into your middle school. Do you have any memories of your teachers, fellow students, or other school employees? If you do, write them down.

| People: | Ways They Wronged Me: | Release Date |
| --- | --- | --- |
|  |  |  |
|  |  |  |
|  |  |  |
|  |  |  |
|  |  |  |
|  |  |  |
|  |  |  |
|  |  |  |
|  |  |  |
|  |  |  |
|  |  |  |
|  |  |  |
|  |  |  |
|  |  |  |
|  |  |  |
|  |  |  |
|  |  |  |
|  |  |  |
|  |  |  |
|  |  |  |
|  |  |  |
|  |  |  |
|  |  |  |
|  |  |  |
|  |  |  |
|  |  |  |
|  |  |  |
|  |  |  |
|  |  |  |

How about high school? Do any memories come to mind? If they do, then write them down.

Think of your time at college. Do you have any unpleasant memories of your teachers, fellow students, or other school employees from your time in college? Write them down.

Take time now to see if you have any other vivid, unpleasant, or painful memories of your school career. If you do, write them down. If something comes to mind later, you can come back and write it down.

If the timer has gone off, stop and pray through each item with the Prayer of Release. Put the date in the last column when you're done praying. Schedule another time to continue and let your prayer partner know.

## *Your Other Relationships*

### Friends and Neighbors

Now think of your other relationships. Think back to your earliest memories of childhood. Do you have any vivid, unpleasant, or painful memories of your friends and neighbors? If anything comes to mind, write their names and what they did to you. You can jump from one to the other.

Move into your school years. Do you have any memories of your friends and neighbors from when you were in grade school? If you do, write them down.

How about middle school? Do any memories come to mind? If they do, then write them down.

Think of your high school and college years. Do you have any vivid memories of your friends and neighbors from your time in high school? Write them down. Do you have any vivid memories between high school and today? Write them down.

Take time now to see if you have any other vivid, unpleasant, or painful memories of your friends and neighbors. If you do, write them down. If something comes to mind later, you can come back and write it down then.

| People: | Ways They Wronged Me: | Release Date |
|---------|----------------------|--------------|
| | | |

## Clubs, Sports Teams, and Churches

Now think of any clubs, sports teams, or churches you may have been involved in. Think back to your earliest memories of childhood. Do you have any vivid, unpleasant, or painful memories from clubs, sports teams, or churches?

If anything comes to mind, write the people's names and what they did to you. You can go back and forth from one person to another.

Move into your school years. Do you have any memories of your time in clubs, sports teams, or churches from when you were in grade school? If you do, write them down.

How about middle school? Do any memories come to mind? If they do, then write them down.

Think of your high school years. Do you have any unpleasant memories of your time in clubs, sports teams, or churches from your time in high school? Write them down.

Do you have any unpleasant memories between high school and today? Write them down.

Take time now to see if you have any other vivid, unpleasant, or painful memories of your time in clubs, sports teams, or churches. If you do, write them down. If something comes to mind later, you can come back and write it down then.

## *Dating Relationships*

Now think of your dating relationships other than with your spouse(s). Do you have any vivid, unpleasant, or painful memories from when you were in grade school? If you do, then write them down.

How about middle school? Do any memories come to mind? If they do, write them down.

Think of your high school years. Do you have any unpleasant memories of your dating relationships from your time in high school? Write them down.

| People: | Ways They Wronged Me: | Release Date |
|---|---|---|
| | | |
| | | |
| | | |
| | | |
| | | |
| | | |
| | | |
| | | |
| | | |
| | | |
| | | |
| | | |
| | | |
| | | |
| | | |
| | | |
| | | |
| | | |
| | | |
| | | |
| | | |
| | | |
| | | |
| | | |
| | | |
| | | |
| | | |
| | | |
| | | |
| | | |

186

Do you have any unpleasant memories between high school or college and today? Write them down.

Take time now to see if you have any other vivid, unpleasant, or painful memories of your dating relationships. If you do, write them down. If something comes to mind later, you can come back and write it down then.

## *Your Job Settings*

Now think of your job settings. Do you have any vivid, unpleasant, or painful memories of bosses, employees, or customers from jobs you had when you were in grade school, middle school, or high school? If you do, write them down.

Think of your college years. Do you have any unpleasant memories from your jobs from your time in college? Write them down.

Do you have any unpleasant memories between high school or college and today? Write them down.

Take time now to see if you have any other vivid, unpleasant, or painful memories from your jobs. If you do, then write them down. If something comes to mind later, you can come back and write it down then.

If the timer has gone off, stop and pray through each item with the Prayer of Release. Put the date in the right column under "Release Date" when you are done praying. Schedule another time to continue and let your prayer partner know.

## *Your Marital Relationships*

### Spouse(s)

Now think of your marital relationship(s) from when you started dating your spouse(s). Do you have any vivid, unpleasant, or painful memories from when you dated your spouse? If you do, write them down. If you've had more than one spouse, list them one at a time.

| People: | Ways They Wronged Me: | Release Date |
|---------|-----------------------|--------------|
|         |                       |              |
|         |                       |              |
|         |                       |              |
|         |                       |              |
|         |                       |              |
|         |                       |              |
|         |                       |              |
|         |                       |              |
|         |                       |              |
|         |                       |              |
|         |                       |              |
|         |                       |              |
|         |                       |              |
|         |                       |              |
|         |                       |              |
|         |                       |              |
|         |                       |              |
|         |                       |              |
|         |                       |              |
|         |                       |              |
|         |                       |              |
|         |                       |              |
|         |                       |              |
|         |                       |              |
|         |                       |              |
|         |                       |              |
|         |                       |              |
|         |                       |              |
|         |                       |              |
|         |                       |              |
|         |                       |              |
|         |                       |              |
|         |                       |              |
|         |                       |              |
|         |                       |              |

Think of your engagement. Do you have any unpleasant memories of your spouse(s) during your engagement? Write them down.

Do you have any unpleasant memories from when you got married to today? Write them down.

Take time now to see if you have any other vivid, unpleasant, or painful memories of your spouse(s). If you do, then write them down. If something comes to mind later, you can come back and write it down then.

## Children/Stepchildren

Now think of your children, stepchildren, or other children in your home. Do you have any vivid, unpleasant, or painful memories of your children/stepchildren/other children? If you do, list each child individually and write down the memories.

If something comes to mind later, you can come back and write it down then.

## In-laws

Now think of your in-laws. Do you have any memories that are vivid, unpleasant, or painful from your in-laws? If you do, list each in-law individually and write down each memory.

If something comes to mind later, you can come back and write it down then.

If the timer has gone off, stop and pray through each item with the Prayer of Release. Write the date in the right column under "Release Date" when you're done praying. Schedule another time to continue and let your prayer partner know.

## *People in the Medical Field*

Now think of your dealings with people in the medical field. Think back to your earliest memories of childhood. Do you have any vivid, unpleasant, or painful memories of doctors, nurses, or other medical professionals? If anything comes to mind, write the person's

| People: | Ways They Wronged Me: | Release Date |
| --- | --- | --- |
| | | |
| | | |
| | | |
| | | |
| | | |
| | | |
| | | |
| | | |
| | | |
| | | |
| | | |
| | | |
| | | |
| | | |
| | | |
| | | |
| | | |
| | | |
| | | |
| | | |
| | | |
| | | |
| | | |
| | | |
| | | |
| | | |
| | | |
| | | |
| | | |
| | | |
| | | |
| | | |
| | | |

name and what they did to you. You can jump from one person to another.

Move into your grade school years. Do you have any memories of doctors, nurses, or other medical professionals from when you were in grade school? If you do, write them down.

Think of your middle and high school years. Do you have any unpleasant memories of doctors, nurses, or other medical professionals from your time in middle and high school? Write them down.

Do you have any unpleasant memories between high school and today? Write them down.

Take time now to see if you have any other vivid, unpleasant, or painful memories of doctors, nurses, or other medical professionals. If you do, write them down. If something comes to mind later, you can come back and write it down then.

## Your Dealings with People in Legal Fields, Government, and Law Enforcement

Now think of your dealings with people in legal fields, law enforcement, or the government. Do you have any memories that are vivid, unpleasant, or painful of lawyers, police officers, or government workers? If anything comes to mind, write the people's names and what they did to you. You can jump from one person to another.

If something comes to mind later, you can come back and write it down then.

## Anything not covered in the previous pages

Finally, write down any other vivid, painful, or negative memories not covered in the previous pages.

Pray through each item with the Prayer of Release. Write the date in the right column under "Release Date" when you're done praying.

| People: | Ways They Wronged Me: | Release Date |
| --- | --- | --- |
| | | |

# Keeping Your Slate Clean

Once you deal with the offenses God brought to mind in the Long Term Offense List interview, you need to keep your slate clean or toxic anger will take over your life again. Your ability to put off "bitterness, wrath, anger, clamor, and evil speaking . . . with all malice" (Ephesians 4:31) and use the tools of kindness, tenderheartedness, and forgiveness (Ephesians 4:32) is tied to staying current with the anger you have toward a particular offense. After you complete your Long-term Offense List, I encourage you to use the Keeping Your Slate Clean tool in Appendix B regularly. You can keep your slate clean by watching these five areas:

- Watch for memories of offenses that come to mind. After you release the offenses you remember, God may start reminding you of others. You should deal with them by praying the Prayer of Release.
- Watch for new offenses committed against you. You need to learn how to recognize an offense when it's committed. You can start by learning God's commands in the Bible about how you should treat your neighbor.
- Watch for the emotion of *orgidzo* anger. You need to learn to recognize when you experience the emotion of anger. When you know you are angry, you need to take time to identify the offense that triggered it and then deal with it properly.
- Watch for the manifestations of toxic anger. Whenever you express bitterness, wrath, vengeance, clamor, evil speaking, or malice, it should be a red flag signaling the presence of an unresolved offense. You should ask God to reveal the offense to you. If you're trying to keep a clean slate, it should be easy to identify the offense that's causing the toxic anger.
- Watch in prayer. Periodically ask God to reveal any anger you haven't dealt with yet.

Use the Keeping Your Slate Clean Interview in Appendix B once every few months to stay current with offenses.

One of the best ways to know if you're keeping your slate clean is by how you treat your enemies. Paul says in Romans 12:20–21, "Therefore, 'If your enemy is hungry, feed him; If he is thirsty, give him a drink; For in so doing you will heap coals of fire on his head.' Do not be overcome by evil, but overcome evil with good." When you properly release offenses to God, you can overcome the evil committed against you with good. You'll be able to love the people who commit offenses against you even though they refuse to apologize.

## Final Thoughts

You can grow up in Christ and be ready for Him to use because God gives you everything you need to succeed. Now it's up to you to make change a part of your Christian life. Remember these words from the Apostle Paul to the Philippians:

> Therefore, my beloved, as you have always obeyed, not as in my presence only, but now much more in my absence, work out your own salvation with fear and trembling; for it is God who works in you both to will and to do for *His* good pleasure. (Philippians 2:12-13).

I invite you to continue your journey with the next book in this series, *You Can Walk in Love: Becoming an Imitator of God.* May God bless you as you follow Him.

# Appendix A

## *The Gospel*

### 1. You have a problem

You have what the Bible calls "sin" in your life. Sin creates a barrier that keeps you from having a relationship with God and from Heaven. Two things the Bible calls sin are lying and stealing. The Bible says, "*Thieves will not inherit the kingdom of God*" (1 Corinthians 6:10), and "*All liars shall have their part in the lake which burns with fire and brimstone*" (Revelation 21:8). If you've lied or stolen even once, it makes you subject to the "wrath" or punishment that these verses talk about!

Fortunately, God loves you despite your sin and wants to have a relationship with you. "For God so loved the world that He gave His only begotten Son, that whoever believes in Him should not perish but have everlasting life" (John 3:16).

### 2. God sent His Son Jesus to pay for our sin

The Bible says in 1 Corinthians 15:3–5, "For I delivered to you first of all that which I also received: that Christ died for our sins according to the Scriptures, and that He was buried, and that He rose again the third day according to the Scriptures." Jesus could pay your sin debt because He was God's sinless and obedient Son. When Jesus rose from the grave, your sin was paid for!

### 3. God is offering you the gift of salvation

However, there is one more step. Just like when you reach out and receive a gift to make it yours, you must receive God's offer of salvation. How do you receive God's gift? By admitting you have sins that need to be paid for and putting your trust in Jesus' payment for your sins as the only way to heaven. When you do this, the Bible says you become a child of God: "*But as many as received Him, to them He gave the right to become children of God, to those who believe in His name*" (John 1:12).

## 4. Take time now to pray

You can receive God's forgiveness and be freed from His wrath by praying a prayer of faith like this: "God, I know I have committed sins, and I need your forgiveness. I believe Jesus died to pay my sin debt. Today I put my trust in Jesus and His payment for my sins as the only way to heaven. Amen."

# Appendix B

## *Keeping Your Slate Clean Worksheet*

"'Be angry, and do not sin': do not let the sun go down on your wrath, nor give place to the devil." (Ephesians 4:26-27)

This worksheet is the follow-up to your Long-Term Offense List. Since completing the Offense List, God may have brought more offenses from the past to mind, and new offenses may have been committed against you. To keep the devil from having a position of authority in your life, you need to release these offenses. So ask God to help you and do your list! Complete this list once every few months or when you feel that you need to work on the process of releasing.

Have you had any more memories surface for your immediate family: mother, father, siblings, etc.? Have there been any new offenses committed by them since you last did your long-Term Offense List? Have you had toxic anger toward any of these people? Why? Record them below:

| People: | Ways They Wronged Me: | Release Date |
| --- | --- | --- |
| | | |
| | | |
| | | |
| | | |
| | | |
| | | |
| | | |
| | | |
| | | |
| | | |
| | | |
| | | |
| | | |

Have you had any more memories surface for your extended family: grandparents, aunts, uncles, cousins, etc.? Have there been any new offenses committed by them since you last did your long-Term Offense List? Have you had toxic anger toward any of these people? Why? Record them below:

| People: | Ways They Wronged Me: | Release Date |
|---------|----------------------|--------------|
|         |                      |              |
|         |                      |              |
|         |                      |              |
|         |                      |              |
|         |                      |              |
|         |                      |              |
|         |                      |              |
|         |                      |              |
|         |                      |              |

Have you had any more memories surface regarding your school career: grade school, middle school, high school, and college? Have there been any new offenses since you last did your long-Term Offense List? Have you had toxic anger toward anyone? Why? Record them below:

| People: | Ways They Wronged Me: | Release Date |
|---------|----------------------|--------------|
|         |                      |              |
|         |                      |              |
|         |                      |              |
|         |                      |              |
|         |                      |              |
|         |                      |              |
|         |                      |              |
|         |                      |              |
|         |                      |              |

Have you had any more memories surface regarding other relationships: friendships, clubs, church, neighbors, or dating? Have there been any new offenses since you last did your long-term Offense List? Have you had toxic anger toward anyone? Why? Record them below:

| People: | Ways They Wronged Me: | Release Date |
|---------|----------------------|--------------|
| _____ | _____ | _____ |
| _____ | _____ | _____ |
| _____ | _____ | _____ |
| _____ | _____ | _____ |
| _____ | _____ | _____ |
| _____ | _____ | _____ |
| _____ | _____ | _____ |
| _____ | _____ | _____ |
| _____ | _____ | _____ |
| _____ | _____ | _____ |

Have you had any more memories surface regarding your job settings? Have there been any new offenses since you last did your long-term Offense List? Have you had toxic anger toward anyone? Why? Record them below:

| People: | Ways They Wronged Me: | Release Date |
|---------|----------------------|--------------|
| _____ | _____ | _____ |
| _____ | _____ | _____ |
| _____ | _____ | _____ |
| _____ | _____ | _____ |
| _____ | _____ | _____ |
| _____ | _____ | _____ |
| _____ | _____ | _____ |
| _____ | _____ | _____ |
| _____ | _____ | _____ |
| _____ | _____ | _____ |

Have you had any more memories surface for your spouse(s), (step)children, or in-laws? Have there been any new offenses committed by them since you last did your long-term Offense List? Have you had toxic anger toward any of these people? Why? Record them below:

People:          Ways They Wronged Me:          Release Date

_____  _____  _____
_____  _____  _____
_____  _____  _____
_____  _____  _____
_____  _____  _____
_____  _____  _____
_____  _____  _____
_____  _____  _____
_____  _____  _____

Have you had any more memories surface for people in the medical field, the legal field, law enforcement, or the government? Have there been any new offenses committed by them since you last did your long-term Offense List? Have you had toxic anger toward these people? Why? Record them below:

People:          Ways They Wronged Me:          Release Date

_____  _____  _____
_____  _____  _____
_____  _____  _____
_____  _____  _____
_____  _____  _____
_____  _____  _____
_____  _____  _____
_____  _____  _____
_____  _____  _____

Have you had any more memories surface for people in the medical field, the legal field, law enforcement, or the government? Have there been any new offenses committed by them since you last did your long-term Offense List? Have you had toxic anger toward these people? Why? Record them below:

| People: | Ways They Wronged Me: | Release Date |
| --- | --- | --- |
| | | |
| | | |
| | | |
| | | |
| | | |
| | | |
| | | |
| | | |
| | | |
| | | |
| | | |
| | | |
| | | |
| | | |
| | | |
| | | |
| | | |
| | | |
| | | |
| | | |
| | | |
| | | |
| | | |
| | | |
| | | |
| | | |
| | | |
| | | |

# Appendix C

## *Group Exercises*

The Ice Breaker tools for these chapters are included in the following pages

# Test Your Mindset

What do you think about these moral issues?

Sex outside of marriage

    OK            not OK         OK sometimes

Lying

    OK             not OK         OK sometimes

Stealing

    OK             not OK         OK sometimes

Revenge

    OK             not OK         OK sometimes

Partying

    OK             not OK         OK sometimes

Cheating

    OK             not OK         OK sometimes

Gossip

    OK             not OK         OK sometimes


What are your views on these social issues?

Abortion

    OK             not OK         OK sometimes

Euthanasia

    OK             not OK         OK sometimes

Capital punishment

    OK             not OK         OK sometimes

Population control

    OK             not OK         OK sometimes

Climate control

    OK             not OK         OK sometimes

Evolution/Creationism

    We evolved     We were created     Both

The Bible

    All true     Parts are true     Just a book

# Big Lies from the Bible

## Group A

Find the Lie

Now there was a famine in the land, and Abram went down to Egypt to dwell there, for the famine *was* severe in the land. And it came to pass, when he was close to entering Egypt, that he said to Sarai his wife, "Indeed I know that you *are* a woman of beautiful countenance. Therefore it will happen, when the Egyptians see you, that they will say, 'This *is* his wife'; and they will kill me, but they will let you live. Please say you *are* my sister, that it may be well with me for your sake, and that I may live because of you." So it was, when Abram came into Egypt, that the Egyptians saw the woman, that she *was* very beautiful. The princes of Pharaoh also saw her and commended her to Pharaoh. And the woman was taken to Pharaoh's house. He treated Abram well for her sake. He had sheep, oxen, male donkeys, male and female servants, female donkeys, and camels. But the Lord plagued Pharaoh and his house with great plagues because of Sarai, Abram's wife. And Pharaoh called Abram and said, "What *is* this you have done to me? Why did you not tell me that she *was* your wife? Why did you say, 'She *is* my sister'? I might have taken her as my wife. Now therefore, here is your wife; take *her* and go your way." So Pharaoh commanded *his* men concerning him; and they sent him away, with his wife and all that he had. (Genesis 12:10–20)

Why did Abram lie?

## Group B

Find the Lie

But a certain man named Ananias, with Sapphira his wife, sold a possession. And he kept back *part* of the proceeds, his wife also being aware *of it,* and brought a certain part and laid *it* at the apostles' feet. But Peter said, "Ananias, why has Satan filled your heart to lie to the Holy Spirit and keep back *part* of the price of the land for yourself? While it remained, was it not your own? And after it was sold, was it not in your own control? Why have you conceived this thing in your heart? You have not lied to men but to God." Then Ananias, hearing these words, fell down and breathed his last. So great fear came upon all those who heard these things. And the young men arose and wrapped him up, carried *him* out, and buried *him.* Now it was about three hours later when his wife came in, not knowing what had happened. And Peter answered her, "Tell me whether you sold the land for so much?" She said, "Yes, for so much." Then Peter said to her, "How is it that you have agreed together to test the Spirit of the Lord? Look, the feet of those who have buried your husband *are* at the door, and they will carry you out." Then immediately she fell down at his feet and breathed her last. And the young men came in and found her dead, and carrying *her* out, buried *her* by her husband. So great fear came upon all the church and upon all who heard these things.

Why did Ananias and Sapphira lie?

# To Catch a Thief

Circle *Y* if you think it's stealing, *N* if it's not stealing, and leave it blank if you're not sure

Y/N     Copying a CD you borrowed from a friend onto your iPod

Y/N     Picking up a dollar you find on the sidewalk

Y/N     Leaving a restaurant without paying for your meal

Y/N     Eating an unopened bag of chips you find sitting on the break table at work

Y/N     Copying a CD you own onto your iPod

Y/N     Quoting someone in a paper without giving credit

Y/N     Ignoring a mistake the bank made in your favor

Y/N     Returning something you only need to use once so you don't have to pay for it after you use it

Y/N     Trying to take someone else's friend away

Y/N     Using someone else's idea without giving credit

Y/N     Using your offering money to go out to eat

Y/N     Meeting the emotional needs of someone else's spouse

Y/N     Keeping the change when a cashier makes a mistake

Y/N     Picking flowers on the side of the road

Y/N     Using coupons to lower the price

# Appendix D

## Leader Guide

This book is a study of Ephesians 4:11–32. Participants can read the material before the group meets, or the material can be taught by a group leader during the meeting. There are also callout boxes that can be used for discussion. The discussion questions at the end of each chapter are for group interaction or personal reflection.

### Chapter 1: You Can Grow
- Opening Activity: Using a whiteboard, ask group members to list where we get our beliefs, such as school, television, etc. The purpose of this activity is for people to think about where they got their beliefs and how much of what they believe comes from the world.
- Read: Ephesians 4:17–19
- Chapter Summary: God gave apostles, prophets, evangelists, and pastors and teachers to help get Christians ready for Christ to use. The second half of Ephesians is Paul's playbook for preparing Christians for use. The first thing we must do to be ready for Christ to use us is to stop living the way the unsaved do.

### Chapter 2: It's Time to Change
- Opening Activity: Have each person fill out the Test Your Mindset worksheet (Appendix C). The purpose of this sheet is to think about their beliefs, not to discuss their beliefs about them.
- Read: Ephesians 4:20–24
- Chapter Summary: When we hear the Gospel, God opens the eyes of our minds so we can understand the truth that can only be found in Jesus and that He is the source of the life God intends for us. Salvation makes change possible but

change only happens when we put off the old, God renews our minds, and we put on the new.

## Chapter 3 Put off Lying

- Opening Activity: Hand out or open to the Big Lies from the Bible sheet (Appendix C). Break up into two groups. Each group must find the lie and then decide why the person lied. The point of this exercise is for group discussion, identifying the lie, and discovering why the lie was told.
- Read: Ephesians 4:25
- Chapter Summary: The first sin Paul tells us to put off is lying. We need to be careful about the idea that lying is okay because lying contradicts the character of God. There is no clear teaching in Scripture that indicates lying is ever acceptable behavior.

## Chapter 4: Put on Truthfulness

- Discussion: How important was truthfulness in your home growing up?
- Read: Ephesians 4:25
- Chapter Summary: We need to replace lying with telling the truth. Telling the truth is important because we have an obligation to Christ's body.

## Chapter 5: Put off Sinning in Your Anger

- Opening Activity: Watch the YouTube video "Snickers Party Commercial"

  https://www.youtube.com/watch?v=NKOnBbleTX0

  This week's lesson is about sinning in our anger. Question: Do you ever get angry when you are hungry? When else are you likely to get angry?
- Read: Ephesians 4:26
- Chapter Summary: The second thing Paul tells us to put off is sinning in our anger. For us to stop sinning in our anger, we need to understand what the Bible says about anger, learn to

recognize when we are angry, and figure out whether our anger is justified or not.

## Chapter 6: Put on Using Anger Properly

- Opening Activity: Watch the YouTube video "Julian Smith—Hot Kool-Aid" -
  https://www.youtube.com/watch?v=NwTsZHGQ6FE
  This week's lesson is on properly dealing with anger. Question: What would you have done if someone asked you to drink the hot Kool-Aid?
- Read: Ephesians 4:26–27
- Chapter Summary: For us to keep from sinning in our anger, we need to make sure we deal with our anger in a timely manner and in a way that meets God's specific requirements. There are two ways to deal with anger: graciously remitting the sin of someone who asks for our forgiveness or releasing the offense to God.
- Closing Activity: Do the Prayer of Release exercise at the end of this chapter. Give everyone plenty of time to go through the process. This exercise is very important because we will use this tool again later in the study. There may be tears, but that's okay. Be sensitive and give people space if they need it.

## Chapter 7 Put off Stealing

- Opening Activity: Fill out the activity sheet "It Takes a Thief" (Appendix C). Ask the group if anyone had 15 "yes" answers. Go down backward from 15 until everyone raises their hand. Talk about the ones you differed on. The purpose of this exercise is to promote discussion and thought, not to confront people about their beliefs.
- Read: Ephesians 4:28
- Chapter Summary: The next sin Paul says we should put off is stealing. There are many ways to steal, and stealing can have significant consequences.

## Chapter 8: Put on Good Work and Generosity

- Have participants take one of the career tests listed on page 101.
- Read: Ephesians 4:28
- Chapter Summary: We need to replace stealing with good, old-fashioned hard work so we can learn how to appreciate what God gives us and have something to give to people in need.

## Chapter 9: Put off Corrupt Words

- Opening Activity: This week's lesson is on words that hurt. Watch the YouTube video "I didn't do it" -

  https://www.youtube.com/watch?v=ZyEL_9oCxL4

  Question: What do you think hurt the mother more, the fact that the girl colored on her tummy or that she said, "Mommy did"?
- Read: Ephesians 4:29
- Chapter Summary: We also need to put off using corrupt words. Corrupt words hurt the people who hear them. Corrupt words are easy to spot.

## Chapter 10: Put on Good Words

- Opening Activity: Watch the YouTube video "Hallmark Commercial with Michael Angarano" -

  https://www.youtube.com/watch?v=XJTF77Xjqlk

  This week's lesson is about words that build us up. Question: Whom did the Hallmark card encourage?
- Read: Ephesians 4:29–30
- Chapter Summary: We need to replace our corrupt words with words that build up the people around us. God gives us words to build up the church and show His grace to the world, but if we're too busy saying corrupt words, we miss out on the opportunity to spread His grace and grieve the Holy Spirit.

## Chapter 11: Put off Toxic Anger

- Opening Activity: Watch the YouTube video "Julian Smith—Truth" -
  https://www.youtube.com/watch?v=DCVrhKGxKkU
  This week's lesson is about toxic anger. Question: What do you do when you are angry?
- Read: Ephesians 4:31
- Chapter Summary: There are six toxic anger languages we use when we let the sun go down on our wrath and give the devil a place in our hearts. We can't help but use bitterness, wrath, anger, clamor, evil speaking, and malice to punish the people we are angry with.

## Chapter 12 Put on Forgiving Like God

- Opening Activity: Watch the YouTube video "Michael Richards Apology" -
  https://www.youtube.com/watch?v=EI5dGM_l9l8
  This week's lesson is about dealing with people who offend us. Question: Is Michael Richards' apology sincere?
- Read: Ephesians 4:32
- Chapter Summary: God has given us healthy tools for dealing with offenses. We can use kindness, tenderheartedness, and forgiveness by remitting the offense of someone who asks for our forgiveness or releasing the offense to God. We need to deal with long-term offenses to remove the devil's place in our hearts so we can start growing and changing the way God intended.

## Chapter 13: Dealing with Long-Term Offenses

Chapter Summary: The purpose of this week's session is to help people decide whether to complete the Dealing with Long Term Offenses process on their own or with assistance. People who have been taught to believe anger is wrong will have a hard time completing this process and may need help. Contact Pastor Tracy at 4gottenbooks@gmail.com if you have any questions. Help group members who are working on their own to find a prayer partner, make a plan, and prepare to deal with their long-term offenses.

## Chapter 14: The Long-Term Offenses Interview

Chapter Summary: The purpose of this session is to complete the Offense List process. Meet again after a few weeks to see how everyone is doing with the process. Have group members talk about their successes and struggles. Try to meet privately with anyone who is having a hard time. If someone doesn't want to do the Long-Term Offense List, don't pressure them. They should do it when they are ready. Encourage group members to put what they've learned into practice.

## What's Next?

Once you've completed the *You Can Grow Up in Christ* book and the Offense List, consider moving on to the *You Can Walk in Love* book. This book explores what it means to love God, your neighbor, and your brother. It then helps you deal with the issues that keep you from loving like you should. You can request copies of the *You Can Walk in Love* book from Pastor Tracy at 4gottenbooks@gmail.com

# Appendix E

Print copies of the Prayer of Release and the Offense List

Prayer of Release

---

God,
You know what _____ did, when _____
                (Name)                          (What he/she did)
_____.
You know how much it hurt me. You tell me in Your Word that I shouldn't avenge myself, so I'm letting You take care of this. I give You the offense, the anger, and the pain of what _____ did. You do what needs to be done with this
   (Name)
person. Thank You for taking the offense, anger, and pain of what _____ did.
          (Name)
Help me to not let this bother me anymore. Amen.

Chapman, Gary. 1999. *The Other Side of Love: Handling Anger in a Godly Way*. Chicago: Northfield Publishing, p. 45.

---

# List Page

| People: | Ways They Wronged Me: | Release Date |
|---|---|---|
| | | |

# End Notes

## Chapter 1: You Can Grow

[1] Spicq, Ceslos O.P. 1994. *Theological Lexicon of the New Testament.* Peabody: Hendrickson Publishers, Inc., vol.2 p. 272.

[2] Ibid.

[3] Ibid.

[4] Zodhiates, Spiros. 1992. *The Complete Word Study Dictionary New Testament.* Chattanooga: AMG Publishers, p. 949.

[5] Ibid.

[6] Ibid., p. 73.

[7] Ibid., p. 202.

[8] Ibid.

[9] Ibid., p. 108.

[10] Ibid.

[11] Ibid., p. 1173.

## Chapter 2: It's Time to Change

[1] Clark, Harry D. 1924. *Into My Heart.*

[2] Zodhiates, Spiros. 1992. *The Complete Word Study Dictionary New Testament.* Chattanooga: AMG Publishers, p. 113.

[3] Ibid., p. 450.

[4] Ibid., p. 120.

[5] "Archaeology and the New Testament | Bible.org." Bible.org, bible.org/article/archaeology-and-new-testament.

[6] Conocimiento, Ventana al. "Did Jesus of Nazareth Actually Exist? The Evidence Says Yes." OpenMind, 24 Dec. 2018, www.bbvaopenmind.com/en/science/scientific-insights/did-jesus-of-nazareth-actually-exist-the-evidence-says-yes/.

[7] Zodhiates, Spiros. 1992. *The Complete Word Study Dictionary New Testament.* Chattanooga: AMG Publishers, p. 1442.

[8] Reed, Richard. 2016. *Illustration: The Dog You Feed.* September 15. Accessed September 14, 2017. http://access-jesus.com/?s=the+dog+you+feed.

[9] Zodhiates, Spiros. 1992. *The Complete Word Study Dictionary New Testament.* Chattanooga: AMG Publishers, p. 1017.

[10] Ibid., p. 1046.

### Chapter 3: Put off Lying

[1] Zodhiates, Spiros. 1992. *The Complete Word Study Dictionary New Testament.* Chattanooga: AMG Publishers, p. 1492.

[2] Johnson, Jesse. 2013. "Is it ever ok to lie?" *The Cripple Gate.* June 19. Accessed September 14, 2017. http://thecripplegate.com/is-it-ever-ok-to-lie/.

[3] 2014. "Lying and truth-telling." *BBC.* Accessed September 14, 2017. http://www.bbc.co.uk/ethics/lying/lying_1.shtml.

[4] Johnson, Jesse. 2013. "Is it ever ok to lie?" *The Cripple Gate.* June 19. Accessed September 14, 2017. http://thecripplegate.com/is-it-ever-ok-to-lie/.

[5] Boom, Corrie ten, Elizabeth Sherrill, and John Sherrill. 2006. *THe Hiding Place.* Grand Rapids : Chiosen Books, p. 105.

[6] Ibid., pp. 106-107

[7] Ibid., p.107

[8] Eman, Diet, and James Schaap. 1994. *Things We Couldn't Say.* Grand Rapids: Eerdmans, p. 96.

[9] Boom, Corrie ten, Elizabeth Sherrill, and John Sherrill. 2006. *THe Hiding Place.* Grand Rapids : Chiosen Books, p. 126.

[10] Ibid., p. 127.

[11] Ibid.

[12] Ibid., p. 134.

[13] Eman, Diet, and James Schaap. 1994. *Things We Couldn't Say.* Grand Rapids: Eerdmans, p. 63.

[14] Ibid., 95.

[15] Paul David Tripp. New Morning Mercies. Crossway, 31 Oct. 2014, August 6.

### Chapter 4: Put on Truthfulness

[1] Zodhiates, Spiros. 1992. *The Complete Word Study Dictionary New Testament.* Chattanooga: AMG Publishers, p. 120.

[2] Ibid., p. 939.

[3] Spicq, Ceslos O.P. 1994. *Theological Lexicon of the New Testament.* Peabody: Hendrickson Publishers, Inc.

[4] Zodhiates, Spiros. 1992. *The Complete Word Study Dictionary New Testament.* Chattanooga: AMG Publishers, p. 241.

[5] Paul David Tripp. New Morning Mercies. Crossway, 31 Oct. 2014, August 6.

[6] Zodhiates, Spiros. 1992. *The Complete Word Study Dictionary New Testament.* Chattanooga: AMG Publishers, p. 6. Ibid., p. 957.

[7] Specht, Charles. n.d. *Dying For The Glory Of God.* Accessed September 14, 2017. http://www.charlesspecht.com/dying-for-the-glory-of-god/.

## Chapter 5: Put off Sinning in Your anger

[1] Zodhiates, Spiros. 1992. *The Complete Word Study Dictionary New Testament.* Chattanooga: AMG Publishers, p. 1056.

[2] Ibid., p. 105.

[3] Chapman, Gary. 1999. *The Other Side of Love: Handling Anger in a Godly Way.* Chicago: Northfield Publishing, pp. 17-18.

[4] David Seamands. AZQuotes.com, Wind and Fly LTD, 2017. http://www.azquotes.com/quote/821516, accessed September 18, 2017.

[5] Zodhiates, Spiros. 1992. *The Complete Word Study Dictionary New Testament.* Chattanooga: AMG Publishers, p. 1055.

[6] Chapman, Gary. 1999. *The Other Side of Love: Handling Anger in a Godly Way.* Chicago: Northfield Publishing, pp. 17-18.

[7] David Seamands. AZQuotes.com, Wind and Fly LTD, 2017. http://www.azquotes.com/quote/821516, accessed September 18, 2017.

[8] Chapman, Gary. 1999. *The Other Side of Love: Handling Anger in a Godly Way.* Chicago: Northfield Publishing, pp. 17-18.

[9] Ibid.

[10] Chapman, Gary. 1999. *The Other Side of Love: Handling Anger in a Godly Way.* Chicago: Northfield Publishing, p. 35.

[11] Ibid., p. 52.

## *Chapter 6: Put on Using anger Properly*

[1] Zodhiates, Spiros. 1992. *The Complete Word Study Dictionary New Testament*. Chattanooga: AMG Publishers, p. 1122.

[2] Ibid, p. 453.

[3] Ibid, p. 139.

[4] Ibid.

[5] Ibid.

[6] Chapman, Gary. 1999. *The Other Side of Love: Handling Anger in a Godly Way*. Chicago: Northfield Publishing, p. 45.

[7] Ibid.

[8] Ibid.

## *Chapter 7: Put off Stealing*

[1] Zodhiates, Spiros. 2003. *The Complete Word Study Dictionary Old Testament*. Chattanooga: AMG Publishers.

## *Chapter 8: Put on Good Work and Generosity*

[1] Sherman, Doug, and William Hendricks. Your Work Matters to God. NavPress Publishing Group, 1987, p. 116.

[2] Kittel, Gerhard, and Geoffrey William Bromiley. Theological Dictionary of the New Testament. Vol. 3. Grand Rapids (Mich.), Wm. B. Eerdmans, 1966.

[3] Sherman, Doug, and William Hendricks. Your Work Matters to God. NavPress Publishing Group, 1987, p. 124.

[4] Zodhiates, Spiros. 1992. *The Complete Word Study Dictionary New Testament*. Chattanooga: AMG Publishers.

[5] Grudem, Wayne. Business for the Glory of God. Crossway, 6 Nov. 2003, p. 76.

[6] Zodhiates, Spiros. 1992. *The Complete Word Study Dictionary New Testament*. Chattanooga: AMG Publishers.

[7] Theological Dictionary of the New Testament - Volume IV)

[8] Sherman, Doug, and William Hendricks. Your Work Matters to God. NavPress Publishing Group, 1987, p. 126.

9 Theological Dictionary of the New Testament - Volume IV).

[10] Grudem, Wayne. Business for the Glory of God. Crossway, 6 Nov. 2003, p. 76

[11] Strong, James. The New Strong's Exhaustive Concordance of the Bible. Nashville, Tn, Thomas Nelson, 2010.

[12] Grudem, Wayne. Business for the Glory of God. Crossway, 6 Nov. 2003, p. 64.

[13] Ibid, p. 65

[14] Sherman, Doug, and William Hendricks. Your Work Matters to God. NavPress Publishing Group, 1987, p. Sherman Ibid, p. 89.

[15] "Occupations and Professions in the Bible - Holman Bible Dictionary - Bible Dictionary." StudyLight.org, 2019, www.studylight.org/dictionaries/hbd/o/occupations-and-professions-in-the-bible.html.

[16] Sherman, Doug, and William Hendricks. Your Work Matters to God. NavPress Publishing Group, 1987, p. 89.

[17] Ibid.

[18] "A Better Way to Train up a Child." Www.insight.org, www.insight.org/resources/article-library/individual/a-better-way-to-train-up-a-child. Accessed 5 June 2023.

[19] Ibid

[20] Grudem, Wayne. Business for the Glory of God. Crossway, 6 Nov. 2003, p. 65.

[21] Ibid, p. 62.

[22] Ibid.

[23] Hendry, Erica R. "7 Epic Fails Brought to You by the Genius Mind of Thomas Edison." Smithsonian, Smithsonian.com, 20 Nov. 2013, www.smithsonianmag.com/innovation/7-epic-fails-brought-to-you-by-the-genius-mind-of-thomas-edison-180947786/.

[24] Grudem, Wayne. Business for the Glory of God. Crossway, 6 Nov. 2003, p. 65.

[25] Sherman, Doug, and William Hendricks. Your Work Matters to God. NavPress Publishing Group, 1987, p. 114.

[26] Ibid, p. 122.

[27] Ibid, p. 127.

[28] Grudem, Wayne. Business for the Glory of God. Crossway, 6 Nov. 2003, p. 49.

[29] Zodhiates, Spiros. 1992. *The Complete Word Study Dictionary New Testament.* Chattanooga: AMG Publishers.

[30] Grudem, Wayne. Business for the Glory of God. Crossway, 6 Nov. 2003, p. 57.

[31] Ibid, p. 66.

[32] Ibid, p. 56)

[33] Sherman, Doug, and William Hendricks. Your Work Matters to God. NavPress Publishing Group, 1987, p. 92.

[34] Ibid, p. 178.

[35] Ibid, p. 181.

[36] Ibid, p. 184.

[37] Ibid, p. 188.

[38] Ibid, p. 191.

### Chapter 9: Put off Corrupt Words

[1] Zodhiates, Spiros. 1992. *The Complete Word Study Dictionary New Testament.* Chattanooga: AMG Publishers, p. 1278.

### Chapter 10: Put on Good Words

[1] Zodhiates, Spiros. 1992. *The Complete Word Study Dictionary New Testament.* Chattanooga: AMG Publishers, p. 62.

[2] Ibid.

[3] Ibid., p. 1031.

[4] Ibid.

[5] Ibid., p. 1469.

[6] Ibid.

[7] Ibid., p. 929.

### Chater 11: Put off Toxic Anger

[1] Zodhiates, Spiros. 1992. *The Complete Word Study Dictionary New Testament.* Chattanooga: AMG Publishers, p. 1157.

[2] Ibid., p. 744.

[3] "BILLY SUNDAY." Jesus-Is-Savior.com, 2023, www.jesus-is-savior.com/Great%20Men%20of%20God/billy_sunday.htm. Accessed 5 June 2023.

[4] Zodhiates, Spiros. 1992. *The Complete Word Study Dictionary New Testament.* Chattanooga: AMG Publishers, p. 1055.

[5] "The Quotations Page: Quote from Frederick Buechner." The Quotations Page, www.quotationspage.com/quote/33044.html. Accessed 5 June 2023.

[6] Strong, James. 2007. *Stong's Exhaustive Concordance of the Bible.* Peabody: Hendrickson Publishers, Inc., Greek 2906.

[7] Zodhiates, Spiros. 1992. *The Complete Word Study Dictionary New Testament.* Chattanooga: AMG Publishers, p. 341.

[8] Ibid., p. 807.

### Chapter 12: Put on Forgiving Like God

[1] Zodhiates, Spiros. 1992. *The Complete Word Study Dictionary New Testament.* Chattanooga: AMG Publishers, p. 1482.

[2] Ibid., p. 685.

[3] Ibid., p. 1468.

[4] Murray, Andew. n.d. *Like Christ: In Forgiving.* https://www.worldinvisible.com/library/murray/like_christ/lc19.htm. Accessed September 14, 2017.

[5] Zodhiates, Spiros. 1992. *The Complete Word Study Dictionary New Testament.* Chattanooga: AMG Publishers, p. 1468.

[6] Ibid.

### Chapter 13: Dealing with Long-term Offenses

[1] Chapman, Gary. 1999. *The Other Side of Love: Handling Anger in a Godly Way.* Chicago: Northfield Publishing. p. 93.

[2] Ibid.

[3] Zodhiates, Spiros. 1992. *The Complete Word Study Dictionary New Testament.* Chattanooga: AMG Publishers, p. 1122.

[4] Chapman, Gary. 1999. *The Other Side of Love: Handling Anger in a Godly Way.* Chicago: Northfield Publishing.

[5] Ibid.

[6] Ibid.

[7] Ibid.

[8] Ibid.

Made in the USA
Monee, IL
16 February 2025

12160838R00125